The Ancient Art of Tasseography

How to Read
Tea Leaves and Coffee Grounds

The Ancient Art of Tasseography

How to Read
Tea Leaves and Coffee Grounds

Kylie Holmes

MOON
BOOKS
London, UK
Washington, DC, USA

CollectiveInk

First published by Moon Books, 2025
Moon Books is an imprint of Collective Ink Ltd.,
Unit 11, Shepperton House, 89 Shepperton Road, London, N1 3DF
office@collectiveinkbooks.com
www.collectiveinkbooks.com
www.moon-books.net

For distributor details and how to order please visit the 'Ordering' section on our website.

Text copyright: Kylie Holmes 2024

ISBN: 978 1 78904 597 0
978 1 78904 598 7 (ebook)
Library of Congress Control Number: 2024931758

A CIP catalogue record for this book is available from the British Library.

Design: Lapiz Digital Services

UK: Printed and bound by CPI Group (UK) Ltd, Croydon, CR0 4YY
Printed in North America by CPI GPS partners

We operate a distinctive and ethical publishing philosophy in all areas of our business, from our global network of authors to production and worldwide distribution.

Contents

Deja Brew: The feeling that you've had this coffee before.
Unknown

You can never get a cup of tea large enough
or a book long enough to suit me.
C. S. Lewis

Preface

Welcome to this book. I am excited to embark on a journey with you, exploring the enchanting world of tasseography. Have you ever wanted to read your tea leaves or coffee grounds but didn't know how? This book can show you.

Tasseography, also known as tasseomancy, tassology or tasseology is the sacred art of interpreting symbols found in tea leaves and coffee grounds. For the past three decades, I have been interpreting tea leaves and coffee grounds. This form of divination has always held a special fascination for me. I have tried different forms of divination, yet the only thing that resonated with me is tasseography readings.

During my research into my family history, I was delighted to learn that female members on my mother's side also practiced this art. When I discovered this, I got goose bumps, and it was like a piece of my ancestry puzzle being put into place. Knowing that tasseography was part of my lineage made me feel comfortable in passing the knowledge onto others. When I use my abilities now, I feel their presence beside me, guiding me forward towards greater understanding.

Tasseography is a powerful tool that can empower anyone, regardless of their background. By using symbols found in tea leaves and coffee grounds, individuals can gain insight into their lives and make meaningful connections. Like reading tarot cards, these symbols have universal meanings but can also hold personal significance. That's why it's crucial to pay attention to the first thing that catches your eye during a reading.

When you connect with your intuition, you activate it, opening yourself up to endless possibilities and imagination. The more you listen to your gut feelings, your intuition, the better decisions you'll make for yourself. Often, this wisdom has been inside you all along, but sometimes it takes a new practice to bring it to light.

As a tasseographer, I take this practice to the next level by tapping into the energy of the person who drank the tea or coffee and interpreting the patterns and symbols revealed in their cup. With this information, I'm given insight to their past, present, and potential future – and this is where the true magic begins. I rely on my own intuition to spot symbols in the cups.

Uncover the art of tasseography, including its roots and instructions for conducting readings. This book offers insight into the world of tasseography and how to gain a deeper understanding of this age-old form of divination in a new age.

Good luck and Blessings.
Kylie

Chapter 1

History of Tasseography

What Is Tasseography?

Tasseography, also known as tasseomancy, tassology or tasseology is a sacred art in interpreting symbols found in tea leaves and coffee grounds. This form of divination interprets patterns in tea leaves, coffee grounds or wine sediments. The term Tasseography is derived from the French word *tasse* for 'cup' and the Greek suffix *mancy*, meaning 'divination'. This is akin to 'divining from the cup'. The saying *Read the tea leaves* originated from fortune tellers who would interpret the patterns formed by tea leaves or coffee grounds to predict upcoming events. The reading of wine sediment is also known as *Oinomancy/Oenomancy (pronounced en-oh-man-see)* and is believed to have started in Rome. This ancient technique was conducted by examining patterns in wine and was performed by a priestess known as a *Bacchante* and protected by *Bacchus*, the Roman god of wine. Oenomancy could be performed by spilling wine on cloth or paper and the resulting stains are studied.

Origins

The origins of tasseography can be traced back to medieval European fortune-tellers who used splattered wax and lead – eventually evolving into reading tea leaves. Historians have reported that tasseography is known to have origins in Asia, the Middle East and Ancient Greece with Middle Eastern cultures using coffee. Modern tea leaf reading began in the seventeenth century after Dutch merchants introduced tea from China to Europe.

It followed the trade routes of tea and coffee and was practiced by both Baltic and Slavic nations. Tea leaf reading is also closely related to the Romani people, whose nomadic lifestyle contributed to the spread of tasseography. Originating from Rajasthan, Northern India, the Romani people travelled and settled across Europe, Asia, and other parts of the world. With them, they brought tasseography, a traditional form of divination that became synonymous with their culture. They would often open tea parlours or provide door-to-door services for Europeans who were interested in having their fortunes read through tea leaves.

According to different historical sources, coffee fortune-telling first appeared in the Ottoman palaces in the 1500s. Arabic coffee is a coffee culture that later spread from Yemen to the rest of the Middle east, Ottoman Empire, and the Balkans.

During the 1800s, tea grew in popularity in the United States leading to the opening of tea parlours. After World War one, women across the country took advantage of this trend and started their own tea parlours, serving light refreshments and even offering tea leaf readings to their customers.

The art of tea reading was often passed down between women from generation to generation. The oldest English book about reading the leaves is *Tea Leaves* by a Highland Seer. Published in the 18th century, it provides readers with a set of symbols to decipher the patterns formed by tea leaves. The book delves into the practices of Scottish Spae wives, who had a gift for prophecy, and how they would peer into teacups to reveal insights about the future.

Tea leaf reading grew in popularity in the Victorian era when travelling gypsies began offering door-to-door fortune-telling-services. In the mid-1800s, travelling gypsies known as Romani people were fully integrated into society and could often be found giving readings in parlours and tea rooms for a fee. With Victorian ladies as the household heads, social gatherings centred around tea became popular and the Romani people were welcomed to participate.

Fortunes in Teacups Postcards by Bamforth

Founded in 1904 in Holmfirth, West Yorkshire, Bamforth was a well-known British publisher of comical postcards. Among their vast collection of cards, some poked fun at fortune telling and specifically targeted the symbols used in tasseomancy or tea leaf reading. These humorous tea leaf postcards were meant to be sent as greetings but could also serve as study materials for those learning about the various symbols associated with tea leaf symbols. The majority of Bamforth cards were not signed by the artists who crafted them; only a few did so. The company's art department was rather small, consisting of only four men responsible for creating most graphics for the firm's impressive collection of over 50,000 unique cards over the span of 90 years. They deliberately adhered to a house style to maintain a cohesive appearance across their entire line of products.

Fortune Telling Postcards by Fred C. Lounsbury

At the height of the postcard craze in 1907, Fred C. Lounsbury of the Crescent Embossing Company in Plainfield, New Jersey was fully immersed in creating popular and holiday-themed chromolithographic cards. He also ventured into unique sets of magical and fortune-telling cards, such as Good Luck curios, Tea Leaf Reading, Palmistry, Dominoes, Dice, and a set called "Good Fortunes as told by Cards."

Today

After more than a hundred years, Tasseomancy has seen a resurgence in popularity. The internet is overflowing with tutorials and guides on how to read your fortune by interpreting the leftover tea leaves at the bottom of your cup. It has even made its way into mainstream media through books and films.

One of the most well-known examples of Tasseomancy is featured in JK Rowling's immensely popular *Harry Potter* series. At Hogwarts, the wizarding school, tasseomancy is taught as part of the divination course in the third and sixth year. However, it is met with a great deal of scepticism and even provides some humorous moments. For example, in the *Prisoner of Azkaan*, when Harry is asked to interpret symbols in his friend's teacup – to which he simply responds, "soggy brown stuff."

The hit TV show, *The Marvelous Mrs. Maisel*, is an American period comedy-drama taking place primarily in the late 1950s and early 1960s. In the final season, there are flashforwards to later decades. Rachel Brosnahan plays Miriam 'Midge' Maisel, a housewife from New York who discovers her talent for stand-up comedy and decides to pursue it as a career. Midge's sudden arrival had a profound and irreversible impact on her parents' lives. They now constantly argue over what to do about their daughter's failing marriage. Miriam's mother, Rose Weissman, relies heavily on superstitious beliefs and regularly seeks guidance from a Romanian fortune teller. She desperately wants to hear that everything will work out, causing tension with her husband Abe. There is a particularly memorable scene where a character visits a tea leaf reader, seeking comfort in the act of "throwing the cups" during moments of vulnerability and despair. This ritual is referenced throughout the story as a source of solace.

In the hit TV show and book, *Outlander*, the symbols in the tea leaves and the predictions from palm reading during the Outlander series premiere foreshadowed the type of journey that Claire would embark on. Without revealing too many spoilers, while Frank and Reverend Reginald Wakefield are completely engrossed in researching Frank's ancestor, Jonathan Randall, through old documents, Mrs. Graham, the reverend's housekeeper, interrupts with a tray of tea. But sensing Claire's restlessness, she kindly offers to have tea in the kitchen with her instead. In *Outlander*, Mrs. Graham was the kind and charismatic housekeeper for Reverend Wakefield in Inverness. On top of her domestic duties, she was also the head of a contemporary druid group that celebrated ancient pagan holidays and offered services such as palm reading and tea leaf readings. Claire eagerly accepts the offer. In the kitchen, Mrs. Graham examines Claire's tea leaves and announces that the reading is both conflicting and confusing. They seem to suggest that she will embark on a journey yet remain in one place at the same time. They also predict that she will encounter various unfamiliar individuals, including her husband. Claire interprets this as a sign that even after six years apart and six months together, her husband still feels like a stranger to her.

Special Teacups for Tasseography Readings

From the late 1800s onwards, designers and potteries have created various types of "fortune teacups". These can be divided into three main categories: astrology, symbolism related to zodiac signs, and depiction of the seven ancient planets. Before long, various porcelain-makers in both the United States and England began crafting their own renditions. Many cup and saucer sets came with instructions printed on sheets, but there were also sets that had written instructions incorporated into their design. These instructions could be interpreted as part of the decoration and didn't require a separate booklet for reference.

The cups and saucers in the astrology-themed tea set were adorned with the twelve zodiac signs and symbols representing the seven planets, one for each day of the week. The cups and saucers used in cartomancy are adorned with images of playing cards that are typically from a 32-card euchre deck, popular in Lenormand style card reading.

Coffee Cup Readings

Coffee cup readings are also known as Turkish coffee cup readings. It involves interpreting symbols created by the residue of coffee grounds in a cup to gain insights into the future. This practice has a rich history, like tea leaf reading, and is said to have originated from Sufi mystics in the Middle East during the 16th century. The coffee grounds they used were coarse and heavy, unable to stick to the walls of the cup.

The practice of reading Turkish coffee cups is widely popular in Turkey and Greece, as well as in Serbia, Russia, Eastern Europe, the Baltic region, and Middle Eastern countries. Coffee Cup reading is known as "Fal bakma" in Turkish.

In 1540, Turkey was introduced to coffee and the ability to grind beans into a fine powder using mechanical means. This allowed for the quick and easy preparation of coffee, as it only needed to be boiled once instead of multiple times to achieve its full flavour. As a result, the tradition of reading fortunes in coffee cups emerged.

How Do You Read Coffee?

For the most visually striking and unique patterns, it is recommended to use Turkish, Greek, or Lebanese coffee as they leave behind a thick sediment. From my own experiences, every society has its own unique customs and practices when it comes to reading the symbols and patterns in coffee cups.

For a reading of your coffee cup, make sure to use a plain white cup with no decorations or designs on the inside. The saucer should also be plain. Once you've finished most of your coffee, remember to leave a bit of liquid and grounds in the cup. Give the cup a gentle swirl, moving it from right to left if you're right-handed or from left to right if you're left-handed. Position the saucer on the cup, then flip the two upside-down. According to the coffee cup readers I've encountered, this is when you should make a wish. Wait for the grounds to settle at the bottom of the cup. This allows patterns and symbols to be interpreted.

Chapter 2

History of Tea and Coffee

Tea tempers the spirit, harmonizes the mind, dispels lassitude and relieves fatigue, awakens the thought and prevents drowsiness.
Lu Yu, The Classic Art of Tea

History of Tea

Tea is the world's favourite drink. According to *National Geographic*, tea is the most popular drink in the world. It has been reported that people on Earth consume approximately six billion cups of tea each day, making it the most widely consumed beverage globally.

The origins of tea can be traced back to ancient China. As the legend goes, in 2737 BC, Emperor Shen Nung was taking a break under a tree while his servant boiled water for him when some leaves blew into the pot. Being an experienced herbalist, Shen Nung decided to taste the concoction that his servant had unintentionally created. The tree happened to be a *Camellia Sinensis*, and the resulting drink is what we now know as tea.

It is uncertain whether this story holds any truth. The custom of drinking tea has been ingrained in Chinese culture for centuries, long before it was introduced to the western world. Evidence of tea containers have even been discovered in tombs dating back to the Han dynasty (206 BC – 220 AD). However, it wasn't until the Tang dynasty (618 – 906 AD) that tea solidified its place as the national drink of China.

One notable fan of tea was Lu Yu, a writer from the Tang dynasty in the late 8th century. He wrote the *Ch'a Ching*, also known as the *Tea Classic*, which is the beginning of tea's documented history. The book, originally published in ten chapters across three volumes, covers everything from the plant itself to cultivation and harvesting methods, tools used, water quality, and techniques for brewing tea. Interestingly, the final chapter suggests transcribing the book onto decorative scrolls for easy reference.

In the late 500s CE, tea was introduced to Japan from China by Buddhist monks who found it helpful for staying focused during meditation. Tea quickly became an integral part of Japanese society, leading to the development of the elaborate and ceremonial Tea Ceremony, which may have its origins in the rituals outlined in the Ch'a Ching.

During the mid-17th century, tea was a rare and expensive commodity that was only accessible to the royal family and wealthy aristocrats. This new luxury from East Asia brought with it a ceremonial brewing and serving process that was modelled after the Chinese tradition. It was customary for the woman of the house to handle the kettle and teapot, pouring the hot tea into delicate porcelain bowls. In 1618, tea was introduced to the Russians, but the Czar did not find its taste appealing. As a result, it was not until the mid-1600s that tea became popular in Russia. When it did catch on, tea was transported through caravans for thousands of miles and was likely the same type of Pu-erh tea that had been traded with Mongolian and Tibetan traders. Pu-erh tea, also referred to as puer, pu'er, po lei, or bolay tea, is a semi-rare variety of tea originating from Yunnan, China. In the Western world, pu-erh tea is praised for its health benefits; however, there exist several misconceptions concerning its taste, production methods, and other characteristics.

In the late 1500s, the Dutch were the first to import tea from China and make it popular. This led to the spread of tea-drinking throughout Europe. The consumption of tea first gained popularity among the upper class in Britain, it was known as an aristocratic beverage and in 1664, the official trade began with the import of just over two pounds of tea leaves for King Charles II. As time went on, this beloved beverage also spread to British colonies and America, and could be found in coffee houses, tea shops, and tea rooms all around London. Eventually, black tea became known as the national drink, as evidenced by its widespread importation which increased from a mere package for the King to 24 million pounds by 1801.

In the Victorian era, tea-drinking became a cherished tradition among individuals of all social standings. It was during this period that tasseography emerged as a practice. After realising the potential dangers of divination techniques that involved interpreting symbols from molten wax and metal, tasseography was seen as a more secure option.

Afternoon Tea

Afternoon tea is a British tradition of serving food and beverage. Anna, Duchess of Bedford, is credited with introducing afternoon tea in 1840. Soon after, it became a popular pastime for the upper and middle classes in Britain to gather in the drawing room or garden at 5 o'clock for a light meal of tea and delicate sandwiches and cakes. This tradition filled the time between lunch and dinner, which was typically served late in the evening around 8 o'clock. During the Edwardian era, afternoon tea became a sophisticated daily social ritual, with women dressing in elegant tea gowns and picture hats and men sporting smart suits. Over the years, new twists have been added to the traditional scone accompaniments. Now, there are scones piled high with cream and jam and given fancy names like finger sandwiches or finger desserts.

High Tea

Afternoon tea and high tea are different rituals and shouldn't be mistaken for one another. High tea was a meal enjoyed by the working-class families after a long day of working, consisting of hearty dishes like pies, cheese on toast, and meats, all accompanied by a warm cup of tea. Nowadays, we refer to this as 'dinner' or 'supper.' Some households may still call this meal 'tea', but the tradition of 'high' tea has faded over time. It used to be served at a high table with tall chairs, hence the name.

Origins of Coffee

Coffee is one of the most popular beverages in the world, enjoyed by millions of people each day. Every day, over two billion cups of coffee are consumed worldwide. For many people, life would seem unbearable without this beloved beverage.

The origins of coffee can be traced back to Ethiopia, where a legend tells of a goat herder named *Kaldi* who noticed his goats becoming more active after eating berries from a particular plant. Curiosity piqued, Kaldi tasted the berries himself and experienced their stimulating effects. This discovery quickly spread and the use of coffee berries as a stimulant became widespread.

Typically, coffee plants have a lifespan of 40 to 50 years, although with proper care, they can thrive and survive for up to a century. There are approximately 25 million families who make a living through farming, and for them, coffee isn't just a product – it is their entire way of life.

The Spread of Coffee

The use of coffee quickly spread to the Arabian Peninsula. There, it was first roasted and brewed to create a popular beverage. These places also served as social hubs for discussions on politics and business, earning them the name 'qahwah houses' (qahwah meaning coffee in Arabic) in cities like Mecca and Medina.

During the 16th century, coffee's popularity expanded to Europe and became a sought-after commodity for the wealthy. In bustling cities such as London, Paris, and Vienna, coffee houses emerged as vibrant centres of intellectual and cultural exchange.

Coffee has long been a unifying force, causing trouble for those in positions of power. During the 16th century, many Italians viewed coffee as satanic until the Pope himself gave it a try. Pope Clement VIII was asked by church leaders to try this "devil's drink" which turned out to be a mistake, as he ended up loving it.

When coffee first arrived in Europe, it posed a significant threat to wine and beer. In response to the growing popularity of coffee, the beer and wine industry launched attacks against it, attempting to discredit coffee and even calling for bans on its consumption. However, their efforts proved to be a futile resistance as coffee's popularity continued to rise.

Politics now is rather like going into Starbucks for a coffee.
Rory Bremner

Chapter 3

Intuition versus Psychic

Intuition is really a sudden immersion of the
soul into the universal current of life.
Paolo Coelho

Some of my students have dedicated themselves to studying tasseography. At first, it can feel overwhelming as they try to absorb as much information as possible on the subject. From my own experiences, you must find 'your own way', one that works for you and yes, it does takes time.

Intuition versus Psychic

Do you ever hear people discussing their psychic abilities or intuition, and how they have a sense of knowing things before they happen? One of the most common questions people ask themselves is whether they possess psychic capabilities.

In my personal experience, intuition is a deep sense of knowing, the voice of one's inner self. It is the internal compass that guides us through each day. Do you ever have a hunch about who is calling before you even glance at your ringing phone? That's intuition. Or when you just know what a friend is going to say before they even reach out to you? That's also intuition. In my personal experience, intuition exists in everyone. It manifests as a small voice inside our heads, a gut feeling, or a sudden change of decision based on that internal instinct.

According to psychologist Carl Jung, individuals who possess strong intuition often possess decision-making abilities that surpass those of the general population. They have a keen sense of foresight and are capable of effectively pursuing their insights. Intuitive individuals excel at generating innovative ideas and offering creative resolutions to longstanding challenges.

At the beginning stages of developing psychic abilities and intuition, it can be difficult to identify each one and understand their meanings. It's also common to not recognise when you are utilising them and have different expectations for how they should manifest.

It is not uncommon for individuals to have vivid dreams that foreshadow future events or situations. The sensation of déjà vu, where one feels as though they have already experienced a current situation, can also be seen as a form of psychic intuition.

Are You Intuitive or Psychic?

Let's examine some instances of intuition versus psychic abilities. With permission, you can hold an object owned by a person to gain insight into their character or the object itself. This is known as Psychometry, a psychic practice. You are at work, and you have a deadline to meet. Suddenly you get the solution. This is known as intuition.

How Psychic Ability Develops

Just like any other skill, honing your psychic abilities requires dedication, patience, and practice. From my personal experiences, it is not something that can be learned overnight. It takes consistent effort and daily commitment to see progress. Before diving into practicing or enhancing your psychic abilities, it's important to take a moment to cleanse your energy, connect with yourself.

Intuition comes from a different part of our brain than our thoughts and worries, so taking time to quiet the mind through deep breathing can help access our intuitive part of ourselves. If you struggle with relaxing or finding calmness within, a good tip is to start focusing on your breath which can give the conscious mind something to concentrate on. Before engaging in a reading or session with someone, it's beneficial to set an intention that aligns with what you hope to achieve. I go into this in more detail in the next chapter.

With each reading that I do, I set the intention that I am "to receive clear and supportive information that serves the highest good of all involved".

The Clairs

During a tasseography reading, you tap into your innate psychic and intuitive abilities. These abilities allow you to comprehend things without using conscious reasoning. Your psychic senses may provide information through visual images, auditory cues, physical sensations, or simply a deep understanding that cannot be explained logically. Frequently, individuals inquire about the methods I use to gather the information presented in my readings for clients. The answer lies in understanding and utilising the four primary channels through which our intuition communicates with us, often referred to as the "four clairs" in the realm of psychic abilities: clairaudience (hearing voices), clairvoyance (seeing images), clairsentience (recognising feelings), and claircognizance (knowing). Clairalience (smelling) Clairgustance (tasting) and Clairtangency (psychometry) are also used. While some individuals may have a natural inclination towards one of the four clairs, it is possible for anyone to strengthen their intuition and explore different techniques.

Top Tips

Follow these tips to continue strengthening your psychic and intuitive abilities.

Start by Connecting with Your Breath.

Conscious breathing helps to move energy throughout your body. Practices such as Yoga and Tai Chi utilize the power of breathwork to enhance self-awareness and connect with deeper emotions. As you tune into your breathing, you can connect with your core self and tap into your inner intuition. Focusing on your breath is a straightforward and powerful method to unlock your intuition. Your breath also serves as an anchor to keep you grounded.

Get Out of Your Own Way

Don't let your mind get in the way. When practicing psychic abilities, it's crucial to recognize whether your thoughts or intuition are guiding you. Starting with open-ended questions instead of ones with only a few possible answers or a simple yes or no can be helpful. This approach allows you to receive the most unbiased insights and distinguishes between your own thoughts and intuitive information. So instead of asking for specific answers, try questions like "Why?", "How?", or "What?" to tune into your intuition and receive accurate impressions without interference from your mind.

Learn to Read Auras

The Aura is a special energy field that surrounds all living beings. It encapsulates the essence of your energy, as well as all your present, past, and future experiences. As an intuitive person, you have probably been aware of auras and their meanings for most of your life. To practice sensing auras, find a white background and extend your hand out in front of it at least a few feet away. Take a deep breath and close your eyes for a moment before opening them to look at your hand. After some time, you should start to see a hazy glow appearing around your fingers – this is your own aura. Focus on what you see; is it expanding or shrinking? This exercise can be repeated weekly until you are able to see auras around others as well. This skill will come in handy when reading energies during tasseography sessions – by seeing the aura's colour and intensity, you'll immediately understand someone's mood and emotional state.

Learn Psychometry

The term psychometry originates from the Greek words 'psyche' which means soul and 'metro' meaning measure. It pertains to the psychic ability of sensing or reading energy from an object. Since energy can never be truly lost or destroyed, every object or place will have a distinct energetic footprint. A person with strong intuitive abilities, can sense and perceive this energy when holding or viewing an object. Try this exercise with a friend by asking them for an object that holds significance to them. Take a few deep breaths to clear your mind and focus on the energy of the object. Ask your friend to confirm any impressions you receive – you may be surprised by what you discover.

Connect with Your Spirit Guides

Spirit Guides are loving beings whose purpose is to guide, teach, and protect us. They are present in all our lives, regardless of our spiritual beliefs. Even if we are not yet aware of their presence through sight, sound, or feeling, they are still there for us. No one on this earth is alone in their journey; we are all connected, guided, and loved by our Spirit Guides. Here is an exercise for you to connect with your Spirit Guides:

To connect with your spirit guides, find a quiet and undisturbed place to sit. Make sure to have a notebook and pen nearby. Set the intention to communicate with your spirit guide.

Take some deep, cleansing breaths and focus on the rhythm of your breathing as you relax. Use your thoughts to invite your spirit guides to join you. Pay attention to any changes in your emotions, physical sensations, and the atmosphere around you.

You may notice subtle energy shifts or receive visual images, impressions, or words in your mind. After a few moments, express gratitude to your guides for being present with you. Take some time to journal about your experience.

Practice Affirmations

Many of my students with strong intuition or psychic abilities often suppress their sensitivity early on in life to feel safe and accepted in the world. Yet as you begin to open yourself back up to these gifts to embrace and develop these abilities, it is important to also create a sense of safety for yourself. Affirmations can be a powerful tool for connecting with your psychic abilities and feeling empowered. They work by reprogramming the subconscious mind and empowering us to change our thoughts and manifest the reality we desire. Here are some examples of affirmations you can use, or you can create your own:

I trust my inner wisdom
I am one with the universe
I am supported on my path
I am open to my divine purpose
I am open to my highest potential

Sometimes...

Occasionally, the most accurate tasseography readings are those that stem from a gut feeling. Intuition is a strong force, and to me, it's that feeling in your stomach that stays with you. Our intuition can greatly influence our life, even without us being fully aware of it and is not to be underestimated.

Chapter 4

Setting the Intention – Being Mindful

People driven by intention are described as having
a strong will that won't permit anything to
interfere with achieving their inner desire.
Wayne Dyer

I first encountered the idea of setting intentions in a meditation class around 1998. We all sat quietly waiting for the session to start. The person leading the group invited us to: 'set an intention' for the next ninety minutes. In that moment, the idea of setting an intention has become a regular thing for me, something that is part of my spiritual practice especially in meditation and in my readings.

What Does Setting an Intention Mean?

Intention setting is a frequent practice in self-improvement and spiritual growth. It is also utilised in professional settings, such as for establishing objectives and creating strategic plans. While it may appear to be merely hoping for something, intention setting goes beyond goal setting; it involves dedication and determination towards a specific purpose.

Intention setting is the act of forming a precise and concentrated mental or emotional intention towards a particular objective or result. It requires deliberate direction of one's thoughts and energy towards a desired outcome, in hopes of improving the chances of achieving it.

There are various approaches to setting intentions, such as meditation, visualization, and affirmations. The key is to determine a specific goal or desired outcome and then direct your thoughts and energy towards it.

When I first heard of intention setting, I immediately thought of the *Law of Attraction* and *The Secret*. While there are similarities between the two, with the *Law of Attraction* promoting the idea of manifesting what you desire, setting intentions goes beyond just material desires. The use of intention alongside your tasseography readings can be a powerful tool for manifesting positive change in your life.

For many people, intention setting is a spiritual practice. However, from my own experiences, one does not have to be spiritual to benefit from it. It is a powerful way to communicate your deepest needs and bring about transformation in your life.

How Do You Set an Intention?

Before conducting a tasseography reading, I always take a moment to set my intention. I ask for only the highest good for all to come through in the reading. It may sound simple, but it's effective.

This helps create a connection between our world and the spirit world, while also making my desires known to the universe. As I prepare for the reading, I focus on what I hope to gain from it and surround myself with objects that enhance my connection to the magic of the universe. Finding a quiet and comfortable space, I light a candle and take deep breaths to centre and ground myself. Then, I call upon my spirit guide team for assistance in the reading. And most importantly, I trust my own intuition throughout the process.

From my own experiences, starting my day with intention is allowing magic into your life. I find when I do this, I align myself with my inner self and connect to my goals and put in motion the actions that need to happen. Setting clear intentions before you do your tasseography reading is the best way to connect with this divination.

Take a moment to relax and centre yourself before beginning this reading. You may choose to close your eyes and invite any spirit guides of the purest and highest intention to join you in this process. Spending time meditating and connecting with your inner self can also aid in tapping into your intuition. This will help prevent doubts, analysis, and fear from clouding your mind as you embark on an intuitive reading of the cups.

From my own experiences, this is highly personal to each individual and develops over time. When you are making a tea or coffee for the person who has come for a reading,

1. State your intentions. When you decided what you want, say it out loud or write it down.
2. Be clear – this is an important step.
3. Make sure you keep your intentions as positive.
4. Keep your intentions simple.
5. Shift any limiting beliefs to one side.

Holding the Space

A Healer does not heal you. A Healer is someone who holds space for you. while you awaken your inner healer, so that you may heal yourself.
Maryam Hasnaa

When I meet with clients, I have a conversation with them. I inquire about their reasons for seeking a reading, what they are hoping to delve into and uncover, as well as any challenges or potential outcomes they may be facing. A tasseography reading is a valuable tool for homing in on what truly matters, away from the distractions of daily life. It offers a safe and secure environment for the subconscious to express itself.

The concept of 'holding a safe space' has become increasingly popular over the years, and I think it's wonderful that many individuals incorporate this into their own practices.

As a hypnotherapist, I have professionally trained to hold the space for my clients. To hold the space, means to fully immerse yourself in the moment and view someone without any biases or judgments. I have also been very lucky to have many experiences of people holding the space for me as well.

How Do We Hold the Space?

People often ask me, "How do we hold the space?" It's a great question. The best way I can explain it is by imagining you're with a friend who is going through a tough time and just needs to let it all out. You listen as they rant and cry, and after they've released their emotions, they return to their usual self. As a tasseography reader, it's our job not only to hold space for our clients but also to create a safe environment for them to open and be vulnerable. More than reading the cups, it's important to truly listen to what they have to say and give them the space they need to share their feelings.

Understanding ethics and learning how to hold space goes beyond simply learning the rules of your profession. They act as a moral compass for your business. My goal is to empower you to have a fulfilling practice that brings out your best and serves your clients' highest needs. Through my personal experiences, I have discovered that having a heart-centred and intuitive approach towards clients creates a safe and welcoming environment that meets their needs. Many of my peers and colleagues also work within therapeutic and psychological models of holding space. As I conducted my own research, I realized the importance of establishing clear boundaries and ethical standards in my own practice over the years. Working with clients has taught me the value of a heart-centred approach, and my training has given me the wisdom to set boundaries that protect both myself and my clients.

Chapter 5

Choosing the Tea and Coffee
for the Reading

Drink your tea slowly and reverently, as if it as
the axis on which the world revolves.
Thich Nhat Hanh

In my nearly three decades as a tasseography reader, I have explored different types of tea and coffee for my readings. However, I firmly stand by the belief that using teabags is not ideal. Even if you cut open a teabag to use the leaves, it doesn't produce the same quality shapes and images as loose-leaf tea does.

Which Tea?
Some teas, such as Taiwanese Oolongs or Chinese green and white teas, have larger leaves that form distinct shapes when brewed. Even black teas have bigger leaves that can create their own unique shapes. Personally, I prefer using smaller leaf teas, like tisanes, as they do not have preexisting shapes when rehydrated in water. This allows for a more diverse spread in the teacup, which is why Rooibos is my top choice. However, ultimately any type of tea can be used for readings since each tea leaf reader has their own individual process.

When choosing an herbal tea for divination, consider your intentions and the specific energies you want to incorporate into your readings. Each tea and herb have its own properties that can enhance different aspects of tasseography.

Here are some teas for you to consider for your tea leaf readings:

Black Teas

Among tea enthusiasts, black tea is a top pick for divination due to its robust taste and dark leaves. The intense brewing of black tea leaves provides a solid foundation for the creation of intricate patterns and symbols. In addition to this, it is believed that black tea has grounding and protective properties, making it an ideal choice for fortune-telling. If you are planning on using black tea for tea leaf reading, it is recommended to go for loose-leaf varieties rather than tea bags. Loose-leaf teas allow the leaves to move freely in the cup, allowing for more defined symbols and patterns to appear. Some popular options of loose-leaf black tea that are suitable for divination include: *Assam tea* is known for its robust and rich flavour, thanks to its large leaves. *Darjeeling tea* has a delicate and floral taste, as it is made from thin and light leaves. *Keemum tea* boasts a bold and smoky flavour, due to its twisted leaves.

Green Teas

Green tea offers a distinct experience for those who want to take their own tea leaf reading to a different level. It has a gentle scent and light taste. While it may not create as bold patterns as black tea, the delicate nature of green tea allows for intricate and nuanced shapes to form. It is crucial to choose high-quality green tea for this type of divination to fully appreciate its subtleties.

Consider trying out different varieties such as Dragon Well (Longjing), a Chinese green tea with flat, sword-shaped leaves. Sencha from Japan with vibrant green colour and thin needle-like leaves. Gunpowder Teas is also a good option to use. The Gunpowder tea leaves are withered, steamed, rolled, and then dried and has a good flavour as well. In Chinese, Gunpowder Tea is referred to as "zhū chá", which translates to Pearl Tea or Bead Tea. Its English moniker, however, is said to originate from an English port clerk who noted the similarities between the pre-brewed appearance of the tea and gunpowder. Another theory suggests that it comes from the Mandarin Chinese phrase for freshly brewed, which, when pronounced correctly, sounds like the word gunpowder in English. Each type of green tea can bring unique insights and symbolism to your readings, adding depth and variety to your divination practice.

Herbal Teas

Tisanes, also known as Herbal Teas, are excellent options for those seeking caffeine-free tea leaf readings. These brews are made by steeping dried flowers, leaves, fruits, and herbs, each contributing its unique symbolism and energy to the divination process. Although they do not contain traditional tea leaves, the diverse ingredients in herbal teas still offer ample material for interpretation. Stir in a clockwise motion to invite positivity and increase self-awareness. Stir counterclockwise to release any negative energy. Some popular choices for tasseography include:

Chamomile for calming and clarity.
Lavender for healing and spiritual growth.
Rosehip for passion, creativity, and emotional insights.
Peppermint for clarity, tummy ache and decongest.
Ginger boosts immunity and relieves nausea.
Lemon Balm calms anxiety,
Echinacea Tea prevent and treat the common cold.
Sage Tea helps with brain function.
Passionflower Tea relieves anxiety and improves sleep.

Magical Tea Blends

While pre-made tea blends are usually created with flavour as the focus, you have the power to concoct your own magical tea blends with intention. By combining specific herbs known for their magical properties and brewing them into teas. Here are some of my preferred herbs and spices to work with and a couple examples of my own tea spells.

Chamomile – Promotes healing and increases receptivity, while also attracting abundance.

Rosehip – Known for its powerful healing abilities and ability to draw good luck.

Ginger – Brings success, prosperity, confidence, sensuality, and a sense of adventure.

Orange Peel – Draws luck and money towards the user.

Cardamom – Ideal for matters of love, lust, and maintaining fidelity in relationships.

Dandelion Root – Useful in dream magic, divination, and spiritual work.

Ginseng – Often used for love spells, beauty rituals, and protection against negative energies.

Hibiscus – Used to attract love, aid in divination practices, and enhance dream work.

Honeysuckle – Draws quick abundance and prosperity into one's life.

Lemongrass – A powerful herb for cleansing and opening one's psychic abilities.

Lemon – Known for its cleansing properties and ability to remove energetic blockages.

Bergamot – Provides protection against evil forces and illnesses, and wards off any magical interference.

Oolong Teas

Originating in Fujian and other areas of Southeast Asia, Oolong or Wu long tea has become increasingly popular. Oolong teas, are a traditional Chinese tea, combines the boldness of black tea with the delicacy of green tea. Its partially oxidized leaves offer a diverse range of flavours and scents, making it the perfect choice for reading tea leaves. As the leaves unfold while brewing, Oolong tea reveals an array of shapes, colours, and patterns that can lend to detailed interpretations. Oolong teas from Southeast Asia have rich notes of nutty, smoky, chocolaty flavours. Oolong tea from Taiwan have creamy, floral, gentle notes. Some popular varieties of Oolong tea for tea leaf reading include:

Tie Guan Yin (Iron Goddess of Mercy): A highly fragrant Oolong with rolled leaves and hints of floral.

Dong Ding: A roasted Oolong with twisted leaves and a smooth, toasted taste.

Ali Shan: A lightly oxidized Oolong with a flowery aroma and sweet, fruity undertones.

Tea experts advise that Oolong tea is best enjoyed when slurped slowly and you must gently pull it through your teeth. By doing it this way, it allows you to absorb the aroma of the tea better. Trust me when I say it can feel strange when you do it that way, yet it does give you the best Oolong tea experience. By incorporating Oolong tea into your practice of reading tea leaves, you can explore a broad spectrum of symbolism and discover intricate meanings within the leaves.

Which Coffee?

Although any type of coffee can be used for readings, the most chosen ones are Turkish and Greek coffee. This is because they are prepared in a way that leaves sediments in the cup. Greek coffee, also known as Ellinikós Kafes, is like Turkish coffee in terms of being made on a stovetop with unfiltered grounds. It may also go by different names depending on the country, such as Arabic, Cypriot, Armenian, or Bosnian coffee. The difference lies in slight variations in the preparation method. Greek coffee is thick and creamy due to its very fine powder-like ground beans. Unlike other types of coffee, it is meant to be savoured over a longer period. On the other hand, Turkish coffee involves boiling finely-ground beans in water with sugar before transferring it to a cup where the sediments settle at the bottom while the coffee is enjoyed from the top. These remaining sediments are used for divination.

Loumidis and Bravo are two of the most popular brands for Greek coffee. While this type of coffee can sometimes be made with dark-roasted beans, lighter roasts are more common. The Loumidis brand was created over a century ago by three brothers from the island of Evia, Greece who had a dream to improve their lives and their families'. Today, Loumidis Papagalos is recognised internationally as a symbol of Greek coffee, known for its quality and trusted name. Similarly, Bravo is also an authentic Greek coffee brand that captures the rich taste and aroma of freshly brewed coffee, adding to the vibrant café culture in Greece. Founded in 1923, this brand takes pride in passing down traditions through generations and offers various forms of coffee such as instant, roasted, and ground.

Traditionally, Turkish coffee is prepared by boiling water with coffee grounds before letting it sit for a few minutes and pouring it into small cups without stirring. The leftover grounds can be used to interpret one's future based on the shapes they form in the cup. To make authentic Turkish coffee, a special stainless-steel pot, called a cezve, is used. This unique method results in a complex and exotic flavour that sets Turkish coffee apart from others around the world.

One well-known brand for Turkish coffee is Kurukahveci Mehmet Efendi, which has been around since the 19th century and continues to be highly appreciated by consumers. Their expertly roasted and ground coffee produces a delicious aroma and taste while also creating a creamy layer known as "köpük," a sign of quality in Turkish coffee. Packaged in an airtight container, this pre-ground coffee offers an authentic Turkish flavour using only Central American arabica beans without any added robusta beans. With Mehmet Efendi Turkish Coffee, making traditional Turkish coffee becomes much easier.

Hisar Kahve was founded in 1928, this company was the first to introduce airtight vacuum packaging for its coffee in Turkey. Like other options, Hisar Kahve offers pre-ground coffee with three different roasting choices: Classic, Double-Roasted, and Mastic Gum Roast. What sets them apart is their unique range of flavours, which may be a bit unconventional for some palates. However, the longer-lasting aroma from their special roasting process makes it a popular choice and the easiest to brew successfully among the three options, making it worth a try.

Chapter 6

Preparation – Your Equipment

If a man has no tea in him, he is incapable of
understanding truth and beauty.
Japanese Proverb

Equipment

The first step is getting the right environment and accessories for your tasseography reading. It's important to have a clear, dedicated space for the reading, so make sure to clean off the table and use a clean cloth as the base.

To make Turkish or Greek coffee, finely ground roasted coffee beans are boiled in a special pot called a Cezve or Briki. To begin preparing Greek or Turkish coffee, it is important to have the right equipment on hand. You will need authentic Greek or Turkish coffee cups with a capacity of around 2 fluid ounces or 60–70 ml. The size of the briki is crucial as it determines the amount of foam that will be created, an essential part of making this type of coffee. A sign of a well-made Greek coffee is the creamy foam known as "kaimaki" which should remain intact when served, indicating proper roasting.

Instructions for Preparing Greek/Turkish Coffee

- First, fill a coffee cup with room temperature water and transfer it to the coffee pot.
- Add in the desired amount of coffee and sugar, if using. Stir well until all lumps of coffee have dissolved.
- Place the pot on medium heat and stir once or twice during the process.

- Before it reaches boiling point and begins to foam, remove the pot from the heat and carefully pour it into the coffee cup.
- Let the coffee sit for 5 minutes to allow the granules to settle at the bottom and for the temperature to cool down.
- Sip slowly while enjoying its rich flavours.

Helpful Tips

- Always start with room temperature water for best results.
- Cooking over medium heat allows for a slower release of the flavours.
- Keep an eye on your coffee as it may boil over if left unattended.
- A small amount of sugar can enhance the aroma of the coffee.
- Avoid letting it reach boiling point, as this will affect the foam and taste negatively. Once it starts to foam, it's ready.
- When pouring, start low and gradually lift the coffee pot higher before bringing it back down to cup level.
- Allow for a 5-minute rest after serving. This will help cool down the coffee and allow any remaining residue to settle at the bottom.

Making the Tea

For the tea leaf reading, select an entirely white teacup with a handle positioned below the rim to clearly see the tea leaves. Opt for a shallow, wide and curved cup instead of a tall, cylindrical mug. In my own experience, tea may not distribute evenly throughout the cup in a cylindrical mug. While some teacups specifically designed for tea leaf readings may have symbols already imprinted inside, this is not necessary and could be overwhelming for beginners. When making the tea, do NOT add any milk, lemon, or sugar as this doesn't help in the reading in any way.

During a tea leaf reading, dry tea leaves are dropped into a teapot and hot water is added. After steeping for 2 - 3 minutes, the tea is poured directly into cups without using a strainer.

Let the tea steep for a few minutes before drinking it. When finished, leave a small amount of tea in the cup, and hold the handle with your left hand. In a soft voice, ask for guidance in reading your future. Then, gently swirl the cup counterclockwise. Next, place a saucer on top of the cup and flip them together, allowing the remaining liquid to drain away. After about a minute, carefully lift the cup from the saucer starting from the right side. Now, you can observe and interpret the patterns of tea leaves inside the cup.

Before the Reading:

- The ritual of reading tea leaves and coffee grounds is significant as it allows you to connect with your intuition.
- Have faith in your intuition.
- Avoid doubting yourself. Let the process unfold naturally.
- Do not rush through the process. Allow it to happen at its own pace.
- Take a calm and thorough look at the shapes and distribution of the tea leaves and coffee grounds in the cup.
- Do not try to force an answer. Instead, observe and let the answer reveal itself to you.
- As you examine the cup, pay attention to how the leaves form shapes and figures. This could be your intuition guiding you.
- Do not feel pressured by time constraints when reading the leaves.

Being Grounded

The phrase "being grounded" is widely used, but its true meaning may not be fully understood by everyone. To me, being grounded means being present in your physical body and having a connection with the earth. From personal experience, I have found that being grounded allows me to feel centered and balanced, regardless of what is happening around me. On the other hand, when I am not grounded, I easily lose my sense of balance. There are various ways to ground oneself, such as participating in sports, taking walks, dancing, or gardening. Personally, walking my dogs every day serves as a grounding activity for me, connecting me with the earth. Additionally, before conducting tasseography readings for my clients, I always meditate to ground myself and prepare for their arrival.

Common Difficulties when Practicing Meditation

Carving out 15 minutes for meditation may seem like a great plan, but when it comes time to do it, you might feel differently. For beginners, starting out can be a frustrating task. Even experienced practitioners, like me, become uninterested in it. Please don't worry; facing obstacles during meditation is common and expected.

Please remember that there is no right way or wrong way to meditate. This means there's no such thing as failing at meditation. Finding your way is key. The goal of any meditation is to focus your attention and be present in the moment, but you may experience the following challenges:

1. Your mind wanders
2. Your restless
3. Can't visualise
4. Feeling anxious

5. Experience uncomfortable sensations in the body
6. Fall asleep
7. Disconnection

This is all normal. I always suggest to everyone to start by sitting in silence for five minutes each day for one week. If you do not manage this, please do not worry. Taking your time is key. Keep sitting in silence until you can do five minutes each day for one week. In the second week, increase the silence for six minutes for another week and so on. In a month's time, you will find that you are sitting in the present moment for thirty minutes each day. Record your findings in your journal and have fun with this.

Why Tree Meditation?

Both Buddhism and Druidism have ties to nature, with Buddha reaching enlightenment under the Bodhi tree and Druids worshipping among sacred groves of trees. From a young age, I have always been captivated by trees. There is a sense of unwavering strength and stability within them that has always comforted me. The woods near my childhood home were my playground, and I would spend endless hours exploring and climbing the towering trees. As I got older, my admiration for trees only deepened. Their majestic beauty and unshakeable presence never failed to calm me in times of stress or anxiety.

By practicing this tree meditation for grounding, you can establish a connection with the natural world and tap into the fortitude and vitality of a tree within yourself.

Tree Grounding Meditation

Prepare yourself by finding a comfortable position in which to rest and take a few deep breaths. Breathe out all tension, negativity and breathe in patience and kindness.

Just allow your eyelids to close... and relax your mind by thinking of something pleasant... Try to let of any negative thoughts, which come into your mind. Visualise them as beautiful bubbles, which float up into the atmosphere and gently disperse into the Universe.

Place one hand on your stomach and the other on your chest. Take a few deep breaths, filling yourself with air slowly.

Relax even more deeply. Imagine, sense, or visualise a white light in front of you, surrounding you and consuming all your lower vibrations. Allow any negativity to pass into the flame.

(Pause for three minutes)

Relax again, even more deeply.

Now, envision yourself in a serene forest or wooded area. Explore the surroundings until you come across your grandmother tree. Sit down on the ground amongst her roots in a designated spot that has been patiently waiting for you. Allow her trunk to support your back, feeling fully nurtured.

(Pause for three minutes)

Intuitively pay attention to any thoughts, feelings, words, images, or ideas that come to you, as they will be part of your answer.

(Pause for two minutes)

Inhale deeply, expressing gratitude for receiving strength, resilience, wisdom, and protection from your grandmother tree. Let these qualities fill your body and heart—every part of you—as you sink deeper into her embrace.

(Pause for two minutes)

Exhale slowly, releasing any tension, stress, or worries. Continue to breathe at a calm pace as you appreciate the beautiful connection with your grandmother tree and all of nature through her.

(Pause for ten minutes)

It is now time to return to the present day. Make your journey back into your body.

Bring your awareness back to your breath... Feel your in and our breaths as they continue to move through and around your body... Feel your hands, arms, feet, legs, your head, your mind, your heart and let your breath guide you back to a full conscious awareness of yourself.

Open your eyes gradually and observe your surroundings gently. Keep the image of your grandmother tree in mind and express thanks for bringing you back to your true peaceful and connected self. Record your experience in your journal.

Chapter 7

Reading Symbols

Tea ... is a religion of the art of life.
Kakuzō Okakura, The Book of Tea

The Cup

(1) ANCHOR
(2) AXE
(3) HEART
(4) PALM TREES
(5) TRIANGLES
(6) LETTER "L"

The Tea Association of the USA
www.teausa.com

Before beginning your readings, it is important to get to know the inside of the cup. Hold it so that the handle is facing towards you. The cup can be divided into three sections: the rim, the side, and the bottom. The rim represents the sitter, while the side represents events soon. The bottom is a sign of things to come in the distant future. Symbols near the handle are more likely to come true in time.

Starting Out

Traditionally, tasseography would have been passed down through family generations. Today, it isn't done that way. Thanks to social media, there are now many resources available like books and online websites to assist you to learn about tasseography, you also may be able to find a course to learn this ancient art online or at a new age shop.

Unlike many other esoteric arts, from my own experiences in teaching this art over thirty years, I have discovered, tasseography relies on your own intuition. Everyone's intuition is different, and no reader of the cups will practice in the same way. I have learned that you must find your own way. The pattern of leaves and coffee stain left in the cup after drinking is used to determine a person's past, present and future.

As you investigate the tea leaves and coffee stains, from my own experience, I see what shapes and symbols jump out at me. Don't worry if you feel, at first, that you cannot see anything. Feelings of being overwhelmed can consume you and you convince yourself that you can't see anything in the cup. That is a normal feeling to come up. When this happens for me, I take a deep cleansing breath and relax. This may sound daft, but I say to myself that I am giving the cup thanks for sharing its wisdom to me and that if there is a message for the owner of the cup, may I pass this on. Nine times out of ten, I see something in the cup and the reading takes place. There have been a few that I have not seen anything in their cup. I always explain that I am not meant to share anything with them as it is not the right time.

Take a few moments to study what you see inside the cup. Tasseography is an amazing way to build trust in using your own intuitive skills. For example: when I see a horseshoe it could mean two different things: a connection to horses, or their luck is changing.

When I am doing a reading, I get images forming in my mind and it allows me to build a story for person that I am with. A flower could mean they love their garden or flowers are being sent from the spirit world. An ant symbol for one client was at the bottom of the cup, which meant they are moving forward in their life. Scattered ants in another reading showed me that the client was spreading themselves to thinly and they were giving their own power away to people who disregarded them. They were also afraid of their own self-belief and doing things for others was a way of pleasing people and not themselves.

I have discovered that when the coffee grinds or leaves land in the cup, I always look to see how many leaves there are, even coffee grinds. I also look at the white space there is in the cup. I look for recurring patterns as well. As they are all factors to consider when looking at the spread in a cup.

I like to share with you that I have had many people come and have a reading with me and I don't get anything for them. This could mean many things. They maybe blocking or holding back. When I investigate their cup, the patterns would indicate that it isn't the right time to have reading with me. I don't charge them as there was no reading that took place.

How Long Should You Leave It to Read the Cups Again?

I am a firm believer that you should not plan to have the cup read often. I always suggest to people that putting at least three months, but more often six months between readings, as it gives time for things to change, grow, and develop, etc.

Chapter 8

Dictionary of Symbols

Yes, that's it! Said the Hatter with a sigh, it's always teatime.
Lewis Carroll, Alice in Wonderland

Sebastyne Young is quoted as saying: "A picture can tell a thousand words, but a few words can change its story," and symbols found in tasseography invoke a glimpse into people's lives. Over time, this divination practice has built up many symbols dating back thousands of years.

During your first time in reading tea leaves and coffee grinds you may feel a bit overwhelmed and don't know what you are doing. That is normal and I know how you feel. Please take a breath and a few moments to centre and ground yourself. Take your time in reading the cup. Don't be rushed by anyone or read the cup in a timely manner. Don't try to force an answer. Observe the cup in depth and let the answers naturally come to you.

An essential part of tasseography is learning to identify the symbols. This comes with practice. Reading your own cup will boost your confidence in reading for others. From my own experiences, I take into consideration the patten of the leaves and coffee stains that surround the cup. I have discovered that many symbols found in a tasseography reading interact with one another. Start with looking at the largest symbols and then work your way around the cup. The number of shapes in the cup is equally relative to the significance of the sitter's phase in life. I have discovered that many shapes in the cup indicates that the sitter is going through a crucial phase in their life. Less shapes indicate that the sitter has less important things to worry about. Another point to observe is if the shapes are spread out throughout the cup or a few are in certain areas. The symbols found in the cup can include letters, animals, lines, and shapes. Numbers indicate time. This can either be days, weeks, months even years. It also depends where in the cup they are. To see the letters of the alphabet in the cup is an indication of a person who holds the letter of someone's first name.

The real of art of this divination is connecting with your intuition. Please note, all symbols have multiple meanings that depend on the person you are reading for. Trusting in your intuition is the best way to read the cup. The first shape or pattern that you connect with is always the most important. Always remember to note down any symbols you find in your journal so you can create your own dictionary that resonates with you. Good luck and most of all have fun.

Here are some symbols to look out for:

A
Abbey – Has a deep faith.
Ace of Clubs – Seeking advice from older person.
Ace of Diamonds – Prosperity.
Ace of Hearts – Tranquillity.
Ace of Spades – Change of dwelling.
Acorn – New beginnings.
Aires – Strong emotions.
Airplane – Projects not going well.
Alien – Feeling out of sync.
Alligator – Feeling anxious.
Almonds – Positive enjoyable times ahead.
Altar – Inner harmony.
Ambulance – Situations will improve.
Amulet – Happiness, health, prosperity, and protection.

Anchor – Success in business. If blurred, doubts are clouding thinking.

Angel – Protection/Good News.

Ankh – Creative power and abundance.

Ant – Social interactions and teamwork.

Ape – Robust, strong, bold, and resilient.

Apple – New beginnings.

Arch – Strength, support, and stability.

Ark – Positive opportunities are in your life now.

Arm – Internal and external struggles.

Army – Facing conflict with others.

Arrow – Moving in the right direction.

Asterisk – Hidden information or fine print that is been overlooked.

Axe – Overcoming problems.

B

Baby – New beginnings/challenges.

Bag – Untapped potential.

Ball – Fun and games.

Balloons – Celebrations.

Banana – Contentment.

Barrel – Abundance, money.

Basket – Addition to the family.

Bath – Emotional cleansing.

Bats – Major changes and transitions.

Bear – Safety.

Bed – Rest is required.

Bee – Become very busy.

Beehive – Happiness in love, and luck in business.

Beetle – A time of spiritual growth and awakening.

Bell – Noisy demands being made.

Bench – Stability.

Bike – A balanced life is required.

Birds – Freedom, travel, news coming to you.

Boat – Visit from a friend.

Boomerang – bouncing back.

Boots/Shoes – Travel, hard work, strength. Take note to which direction the boot/shoe is pointing.

Bottle – Temptations offered.

Bouquet – Luck, joy, hope.

Box – You are about to receive a gift.

Bracelet – Personal commitment/bond that you have with someone.

Branch of a tree – Reaching out to someone/ olive branch.

Branch of a tree – Symbolises family, grandchildren.

Bricks – Individual ideas, thoughts, plans that will shape your future.

Bridge – Journey's to be taken.

Bridge – A transition to new things/ Spiritual connection.

Broom – Changes in life are coming, sweeping out the old, bringing in the new.

Broom – Spiritual cleansing and renewal.

Broken Heart – Overwhelming emotions.

Bull – Stubbornness, strong will, strength, power.

Bus – Journey to new places or a new level of understanding.

Butterfly – Freedom.

Butterfly – Transformation.

C

Cage – Feeling imprisoned, suppressed emotions.

Camel – Carrying burdens.

Candle – Connecting with your inner voice.

Canoe – Reach for goals in your life.

Car – Travel.

Caravan – Desire to break away from the norm and explore new things.

Carriage – Rebirth and regeneration.

Cart – Moving forward and achieving goals.

Castle – Unexpected money.

Cat – Secrets shared.

Chain – Engagements, Weddings, christenings.

Chair – Material wealth. Stillness and quiet contemplation.

Chicken – A desire for fulfilment and satisfaction.

Cigar – Choices, new experiences, openness.

Cigarette – Relaxation needed. Take a break.

Circle – A completion of tasks. Protection.

Clock – Feeling time is running out.

Cloud – Movement.

Clover/Four leaf clover – good luck /prosperity.

Clown – Fun needed in life.

Coffin – New beginnings and the end of a troublesome period.

Coin – Saving money.

Compass – Finding direction in life.

Cow – Prosperity.

Crab – Satisfaction.

Crescent – Receiving news.

Cross – Spiritual beliefs, protection.

Crown – Success coming your way.

Cup – Celebration

Cylinder – Creativity and inspiration.

D

Daffodil – Symbol of hope and new beginnings.

Dagger/Knife/Sword – Risks may be taken.

Daisy – Positivity.

Dart – Accuracy and precision in one's goals.

Dashes – Keeping busy.

Deer – Gentleness, happiness, harmony, power, longevity, and peace.

Desk – Business meetings.

Dinosaur – Symbolic of inner strength and power.

Dog – Loyalty, have good friends.

Dolphin – Open up to your emotions.

Donkey – Time to be patient.

Door – New opportunities.

Dots – Can forecast of an upcoming increase or flurry of activity.

Dragon – Changes.

Drum – Rhythm, power, and energy.

Duck – False gossip.

E

Eagle – Success and soaring over obstacles.

Egg – New beginnings. Fertility.

Elephant – Strength – carrying the weight of the world on your shoulders.

Envelope – Good news is coming.

Eye – Seeing beyond the veil.

F

Face – Changes are coming.

Fan – Take time out for relaxation.

Fairy – Inner wisdom and healing.

Feathers – Spiritual progress.

Feet – Decisions need to be made.

Fences – Limitations, minor setbacks.

Fern – A need for creative solitude.

Finger – Extra care needs to be taken.

Fire – Passion, transformation.

Fish – Wisdom.

Flag – Compromising your integrity.

Flower – Spiritual growth, gifts, nature spirits.

Fly – An annoying person.

Fork – Expansion.

Fountain – Steer clear of negative thoughts.

Fox – Caution should be taken when dealing with friends.

Frog – A cleansing time.

Fruit – Prosperity.

G

Gate – Opportunities will come.

Gemini – Symbolises twins, quick thinking, witty.

Giant – Obstacles and challenges that must be overcome.

Glass – Dissatisfaction with life.

Goat – Stubbornness.

Grapes – Good health, happiness.

Grasshopper – Happiness, pride, resourcefulness.

Griffin – A need to stand up for yourself.

Gun – Control, power, fear, aggression, and anger.

H

Hammer – Overcoming challenges.

Hand – A helping hand.

Handcuffs – Feeling restrained, trapped, or powerless.

Hare – Friendship.

Hare – Rebirth of an idea.

Harp – Healing and harmony.

Harp – Spiritual growth and inner peace.

Hat – Improvements. A new job.

Hawk – Take a step back from everything.

Head – Overthinking.

Heart – Love, family relationships, harmony.

Hen – Additions to the family.

Hill – Spiritual challenges and obstacles.

Horn – Gossip.

Horse – Galloping forward in life. Good news.

Horseshoe – Make a wish.

Hourglass – Time is ticking and something important requires your attention.

House – Success, stability.

Human figures – Devoted friends.

Hurdles – Hurdles will be overcome, you're on the right track.

I

Iceberg – Emotions are bigger than they appear.

Igloo – Take time out.

Insect – Negative thinking/feeling.

Ivy – Twists and turns.

J

Javelin – Aiming high.

Jaw – Gossip.

Jug – Health.

K

Kangaroo – Can't sit still.

Kettle – Minor delays.

Key – Problems solved, Business improvements.

Kite – Make a wish.

Knots – Anxiety/ Stress.

L

Ladder – Growth and reward from determination.

Ladybird – Getting good news.

Lamb – Gentleness.

Lamp – Secrets revealed.

Lantern – A light shining on current issues.

Leaf – Changes are coming.

Leg – Moving forward.

Lemon – Bitterness.

Letters of the alphabet – First initial of a forename.

Lighthouse – Guidance from spirit.

Lightning bolt – Need more energy.

Lily – True friends.

Lines – A journey or being chained to something that isn't good for you.

Lion – Powerful friends.

Lock – Obstacles will be overcome.

M

Man – Arrival of visitors.

Medal – Seeking approval.

Mermaid – The pursuit of something unattainable.

Monster – Lack of self-belief in oneself.

Moon – Shows success and reflection of self.

Mountain – Overcome difficulties.

Mouse – Take small steps and everything will fall into place.

Mushroom – Growth.

N

Nail – Injustice, unfairness.

Necklace – Hope, unity, fairness.

Nest – Saving money for house improvements.

Net – A symbol of your own actions.

O

Oats – Warmth and comfort.

Octopus – Warning.

Ostrich – Sticking head in the sand.

Oval – Completion.

Owl – Gaining greater wisdom.

Ox – Finding inner strength.

Oyster – Moving forward in life.

P

Palm Tree – Success.

Pan – Anger towards a situation.

Parachute – Breaking free from negative patterns.

Parasol – Protection and shelter.

Parrott – Learning new skills and opportunities.

Parrot – Gossip.

Path – Taking direction in life.

Pear – Potential and possibilities.

Pear – Blessings.

Pencil – Creativity.

Pentagon – Power, control, and authority.

Piano – A need for self-expression.

Pig – Jealousy and gluttony.

Prawn – Flexibility and creativity in your way of thinking.

Pumpkin – Prosperity.

Puppy – Feeling playful and happy.

Pyramid – Inner growth.

Q

Quail – Changes will soon manifest in your life.

Question Mark – open to new things.

Quill – Spiritual progression.

Quince – Competition at work.

R

Rabbit – Shy, timid person.

Racket – Get moving, lack of energy.

Racquet – Inner battles with self.

Raft – Making a fresh start.

Rainbow – Luck, hope, fortune, and wishes are coming true.

Rake – Part of life needs sorting out.

Rat – Deceit.

Ring – Commitment.

Road – Journey will be taken.

Rooster – Courage and determination.

S
Saddle – Control in your personal life.

Satchel – Carrying something important.

Satellite – Spiritual communication.

Saw – Feeling cut off.

Scales – Justice.

Scissors – Separation.

Shark – Feeling out of depth.

Sheep – Peace.

Shell – You will find a simple treasure.

Ship – Upcoming journey.

Snake/Serpent – Negativity.

Spider – Creativity.

Spiral – Power.

Square – Feeling boxed in.

Stairs – Physical or emotional barriers that need to overcome in life.

Star – Wishes granted.

Stork – News about the family.

Sun – Success and happiness entering your life.

Swan – Finding a soulmate for life.

Sword – Disputes.

T
Table – Family connections.

Tap – Feeling emotional.

Teapot – Family relationships.

Teddy Bear – Events that currently affect you in life.

Teeth – Money issues.

Telescope – Looking at things from a different perspective.

Thumb – Strength, power, independence, and control.

Toad – Transformation.

Torch – Connection to your spiritual source.

Tortoise – A strong will to succeed.

Train – Opportunities coming your way.

Tram – Movement and transition.

Tree – Growth. A grounded person.

Triangles – Luck on your side.

Tripod – Progress towards your goals.

U

Udder – Fertility.

Umbrella – Annoyances. Sheltering from jealously.

Unicorn – Magical times ahead.

Urn – Holding onto feelings.

V

V – Roman numeral representation of number 5.

Violin – New beginnings.

Volcano – Outbursts of anger.

Vulture – Negativity.

W

Wagon – Progress and movement.

Wand – Good news.

Wasp – Angry feelings.

Wavy lines – Unsure, frustrations.

Whale – Protection, power, peaceful communication.

Wheel – Change, progress.

Windmill – Guard against your scattered energies.

Window – A desire for a new perspective or a longing for change.

Wings – Guardian, spirituality.

Witch – Sensitivity and intuition that is not allowed natural expression.

Wizard – Great power and wisdom.

Wolf – Spiritual guardian.
Worms – Rivals.

X
X Letter – Bringing in balance, your goals are in sight.
Xylophone – Harmony.

Y
Yacht – Travel plans need to be made.
Yak – Spending time alone.

Z
Zebra – New opportunities.
Zig-Zag – Erratic behaviour.
Zip – Feeling stuck.
Zombie – Feeling out of touch with oneself.

Chapter 9

Teas and Coffee for the Wheel of the Year

Tea! Bless ordinary everyday afternoon tea!
Agatha Christie

What Are the Sabbats?

The Wheel of the Year is a significant symbol for pagans, Wiccans, and witches as it represents the eight festivals that hold great importance to them. These occasions, known as Sabbats, adhere to a nature-based schedule consisting of four solar holidays and four seasonal celebrations in between. Due to their connection to precise astronomical moments, the solstices and equinoxes may vary slightly from year to year.

Paganism is a broad and varied community with a focus on practices such as ecology, witchcraft, Celtic beliefs, and certain gods and goddesses. The core belief of many pagans is acknowledging the divinity in nature, which influences their celebrations throughout the year based on their understanding of the natural world.

It is your choice whether to observe the festivals on the Wiccan calendar, and how you choose to do so is entirely up to you. If you are a member of a coven, there may be established rituals and customs for each holiday that you and your fellow witches will partake in. However, if you practice alone, take the opportunity to educate yourself about each Sabbat and discover the traditional colours, foods, and decorations associated with each one.

The Wheel of the Year Festivals are:

- Yule: December 19–23
- Imbolc: February 1–2
- Ostara: March 19–23
- Beltane: April 30 – May 1
- Litha/Midsummer: June 19–23
- Lughnasadh: August 1–2
- Mabon: September 20–24
- Samhain: October 31 – November 1

While *Yule, Ostara,* and *Samhain* may be the most well-known, there are numerous other celebrations throughout the year that hold great significance to witches, wiccans, and pagans.

The eight sabbats are divided into two categories: the lesser and greater sabbats. The lesser sabbats, which include *Yule, Ostara, Litha,* and *Mabon,* correspond to the solstices and equinoxes of the pagan seasonal calendar. On the other hand, *Imbolc, Beltane, Lammas,* and *Samhain* are considered the greater sabbats, marking the midpoint of each season. With a celebration every six weeks, there is always something to anticipate in the pagan community. Each sabbat has its own unique spells, rituals, and beverages associated with it.

Yule: December 19–23

Yule is the celebration of the winter solstice, marking the shortest day and longest night of the year. Though it may be a time of darkness, it is also a time of new beginnings, as light will soon enter the world once again. Yule is a time for introspection and contemplation, reflecting on the events of the past year. It's also a time to honour and remember loved ones who have passed on, inviting them to join in the festivities. One important tradition during this sabbat is the burning of the Yule log throughout the night, symbolizing how even in the darkest times, there will always be light. A piece of the log is saved for the following year, representing the ongoing cycles of nature.

Yule Spiced Tea

Ingredients:
1 litre of water
9oz of Black tea
2 cinnamon sticks
2 teaspoons of ground nutmeg
A small piece of fresh ginger
½ an orange

Method: Cut the ginger into thin strips and slice the orange into rounds. If you are using loose leaf tea, pack it into a separate infuser or reusable tea bag. Place all the ingredients in a pot and cover with boiling water. Let it steep for five minutes before removing the tea. Then let it steep for an additional five minutes before pouring.

Imbolc: February 1–2

Imbolc, also known as Candlemas, marks the midpoint of winter and is a time for renewal and clearing out the old to make space for the new. This fire festival celebrates Brigid, the Celtic goddess of motherhood and fertility, through the making and burning of a sun wheel or Brigid's Cross. As we honour Brigid, we are reminded to let go of things that no longer serve us and embrace creativity in preparation for the upcoming season of growth. Use this time to clean and organize your physical environment, as well as clear your mind and heart of anything holding you back. Let Imbolc be a reminder of the continuity of life and the endless possibilities that await us.

Cinnamon and Ginger Tea

Ingredients:
2 cinnamon sticks
¾ cup (40g) ginger, chopped and peeled
1 cup of water
Honey to taste

Method: Pour the water into a saucepan. Add the ginger. Add the cinnamon stick. Let these ingredients "cook" for about 10 minutes over low heat. Remove the pot from the heat and pour the honey into the mixture.

Ostara: March 19–23

Ostara, observed on the first day of spring, symbolizes the balance between light and darkness. This holiday is attributed to Eostre, the Germanic goddess of dawn. It is a time for new beginnings, abundance, and limitless potential. On the spring equinox, day and night are equal in length. As the days grow longer, the aspirations and goals set during Imbolc may come to fruition.

Rosemary Tea

Ingredients:
Fresh rosemary sprigs
Honey (Agave Syrup for vegans)
Lemon Wedge

Method: Place several sprigs of rosemary into a teapot and pour boiling water over them. Let it steep for five minutes. To balance out the strong rosemary flavour, stir in honey or agave and a squeeze of lemon juice. This is an important step to get the best flavour, otherwise the rosemary is too overpowering.

Beltane: April 30–May 1

Beltane, also called May Day, marks the midway point between spring and summer. As the sun shines brightly on nature, life bursts forth from the ground. This sabbat is associated with passion, love, and sexuality. It's customary to have hand-fasting ceremonies during Beltane, where two individuals have their hands bound together as a symbol of their commitment to one another. As they exchange vows, they are also connected physically. Bonfires are a popular tradition during this time, and jumping over the flames is believed to bring blessings while sending animals through the smoke can protect them. The maypole, adorned with greenery and ribbons, is another well-known feature as it stands tall for coven members to dance around.

Mint Chamomile Tea Recipe

Gathering chamomile flowers and mint from your own garden will result in a tea that cannot be replicated with store-bought and dried ingredients.

Prep: 5 minutes
Cook: 5 minutes
Total: 10 minutes

Ingredients:
3–4 tablespoons fresh chamomile flowers
1 small, fresh sprig of mint
8 ounces boiling water.

Method: Grab an infuser teapot and fill it with a handful of fragrant chamomile flowers. Next, take a few sprigs of fresh mint and gently roll them between your hands to release their oils. Measure out 8 ounces of water and pour it into the teapot, then put it on medium heat. Allow the water to come to a boil before letting the chamomile and mint steep for five minutes.

Litha/Midsummer: June 19–23

Known as Litha or Midsummer, this sabbat marks the summer solstice – the longest day and shortest night of the year. It is a time to rejoice in the triumph of light before it begins to wane and give way to autumn. Nature is at its fullest with abundant crops, flourishing plants, and thriving wildlife. This is also when the Sun God descends until his rebirth at Yule. It is a moment to reflect on all that has come and express gratitude while seeking continued prosperity for the upcoming season. The warmth of the sun's light is celebrated before it ultimately gives way to darkness. Bonfires are often lit during this time to symbolize the sun's strength, and some will stay up all night to witness the sunrise in honour of this revered celestial body.

Summer Solstice Tea

Ingredients:
1 Tablespoon organic rose petals, fresh or dried
1 teaspoon organic spearmint fresh or dried
1 teaspoon organic lemongrass fresh or dried
1 teaspoon organic lemon balm

Method: Gather all the herbs, whether they are calm and dried. Place them in a tea infuser or tea bag. Boil some water and pour 2 cups over the herbs. Let it steep for 3–5 minutes before straining and serving. This recipe yields enough for two cups of fragrant herbal tea.

Lughnasadh: August 1–2

Lughnasadh, also known as Lammas, is a celebration that falls halfway between summer and autumn. It serves as the final farewell to the warm season and a reminder to start preparing for colder weather ahead. Additionally, it marks the first harvest of the year, typically consisting of grains.

Ancient Pagans observed this sabbat with both hope and fear – hoping for a plentiful harvest but fearing that it may not be enough to sustain them through the winter. This time is meant to acknowledge and embrace the changing of seasons. Traditionally, Lammas is celebrated with bonfires, dancing, and feasting. A common practice is to offer the first fruits of the season to the gods and goddesses as a sign of gratitude and to ensure blessings for the upcoming year.

Honey and Elderflower Tea

Ingredients:
1 teaspoon dried elderflowers
8oz boiling water.
1 tablespoon of honey
1 teaspoon freshly squeezed lemon juice.

Method: Boil 8 ounces of water in a kettle or on the stove. Use a tea infuser or tea bag to hold 1 teaspoon of dried elderflowers. Put the elderflower tea infuser or tea bag in a mug. Pour the boiling water over the elderflower tea and let it steep for 5 minutes. Remove the elderflower tea infuser or tea bag and mix in 1 tablespoon of honey until it dissolves completely. Add 1 teaspoon of freshly squeezed lemon juice and stir well. Enjoy the Honey and Elderflower Tea hot or chill it with ice for a refreshing summer beverage. To increase sweetness, add more honey to taste.

Mabon: September 20–24

Mabon marks the final harvest of the year, a time to acknowledge the abundance of summer shifting into the stillness of winter. It falls on the autumn equinox, representing a balance between light and dark as darkness begins to overtake the light. The focus of this sabbat is giving thanks, taking time to reflect on what blessings you have received and considering what seeds of ideas you can plant for the upcoming year. Use this opportunity to set intentions for letting go of unhealthy habits, relationships, or beliefs as the Wheel of the Year ends. Embrace balance as you prepare for another seasonal transition.

Apple Tea

Ingredients:
4 cups of hot black tea
4 cups of boiling water
4 tablespoons of raw sugar or more for taste
1 large apple – peeled, cored, and quartered.

Method: Begin by peeling an apple and boiling water for tea. Once the tea is made, pour it into cups with large rims, filling them about halfway. Dilute the tea with freshly boiled water until it turns a golden colour. Add a tablespoon of sugar to each cup. Finally, place a quarter of an apple in each cup, stir, and serve immediately.

Samhain: October 31–November 1

I love this time of year and this Sabbat as it's also my birthday. Samhain is a significant sabbat for many as it symbolises the beginning of the cyclic Wheel of the Year. During this time, the veil between worlds is at its thinnest, allowing lost loved ones and ancestors to pass into our realm. It's a day to honour those who have passed on. I do this by setting an extra place at our Samhain feast and sharing stories and memories about them. Why not take this opportunity to set intentions and goals for the upcoming year, as well as making room in your life for rest during the approaching winter.

Oolong Loose Tea

Ingredients:
1 tablespoon of pumpkin seeds
1 tablespoon of cranberries
1 cinnamon stick

Method:
Add the listed ingredients into a tea pot and carefully pour hot water over them. Let it steep for two minutes before adding the cinnamon stick, then let it stand for an additional two minutes. Serve right away.

Chapter 10

Teas and Coffee for the Chakras

Every moment, your 114 chakras are creating tiny magnetic fields around you. Your job is to align your 114 chakras and get aligned with the universe to manifest your dreams.
Amit Ray, The Science of 114 Chakras in Human Body

What Are the Chakras?

The Sanskrit word "chakra" translates to "wheel" or "vortex". These powerful centres were first described by Indian yogis as channels for the universal life force energy. There are seven main chakras that run along the spine, starting at the base, and ending at the crown on top of the head. Each chakra is associated with specific organs in the body and influences various aspects of our lives: physical, emotional, mental, and spiritual. There are also chakra points in the hands and feet, which can be activated by placing crystals in the palm of your hand. This can help develop an ability to sense subtle energies. The foot chakras play a vital role as they send signals throughout the body when we step into a hot bath or cold sea, allowing us to ground ourselves to Mother Earth and stabilise our auric field.

Chakras can be visualised as spinning wheels, each one rotating at a different speed. The lower chakras typically move slower than the higher ones, which is normal for all individuals. Closing my eyes, I see my own chakras as spinning rods, whirling in a swift clockwise motion. However, some are moving slowly in an anti-clockwise direction. Using a pendulum, I work to identify which chakra is imbalanced so I can take the necessary steps to restore my inner healing. Each chakra is associated with specific decisions we make in our lives – thoughts, emotions, and experiences that shape us into who we are. As we grow from childhood to adulthood, our chakras develop based on our life experiences. When they are in harmony and balance, we feel healthy and at peace. But when they become unbalanced, we can feel out of sync and drained of energy. This imbalance also affects the flow of energy throughout our bodies.

The Seven Major Chakras

Chakra	Colour	Body Location	Body Location
Base	Red	Physical Body	Base of Spine
Sacral	Orange	Emotional Body	Below Naval
Solar Plexus	Yellow	Mental/Intellectual	Body Above Naval
Heart	Pink	Astral Body	Centre of Chest
Throat	Blue	Etheric Body	Base of Throat
Third Eye	Purple	Celestial Body	Centre of Forehead
Crown	White/Clear	Etheric Body	Whole top of Head

Base/Root Chakra: Muladhara

The name for this chakra is called *Muladhara*, which directly translates to "root" and "support. The purpose of this chakra is to bind your bodily energy with that of the Earth's. Essentially, it serves as a grounding force. This chakra is also responsible for ensuring your basic survival needs are met. These include breathing, consumption, resting, and feeling safe in your physical surroundings. The colour of this space is a bold red, representing emotions like anger, survival instincts, and passion. For a root chakra boost, try brewing some cinnamon spiced tea or dandelion tea, ginger, or elderflower tea.

Sacral Chakra: Svadhisthana

Svadhisthana, the sacral chakra, derives its name from the Sanskrit word for "sweetness" and resides just below the navel. This energy centre is closely connected to creativity and sexuality, as well as one's ability to process and understand emotions, both personal and external. Represented by the colour orange, this chakra can be balanced with the consumption of Fennel tea. Feeling uninspired? A cup of fennel tea may help tap into your creative potential. Calendula and hibiscus tea is also good.

Solar Plexus Chakra: Manipura

The Manipura chakra, also known as the solar plexus, is associated with confidence, self-esteem, and personal power. Located in the stomach area, it is often represented by the colour yellow and symbolizes a "city of jewels" or a "lustrous gem" in Sanskrit. If you're feeling stuck or lacking direction, try drinking Ginger or Turmeric tea to help you find your way forward. Rosemary, fennel, and cinnamon tea is also good.

Heart Chakra: Anahata

Anahata, the heart chakra, translates to "unhurt" in Sanskrit. Positioned between the lower and upper chakras, it resides at the centre of the chest. This vital energy centre serves as a bridge between our emotions and our mind and soul. It is where love flows from and is stored. The colour associated with the heart chakra is green, and consuming rose tea is said to aid in healing a broken heart. Jasmine tea is also good.

Throat Chakra: Vishuddha

Located in the throat, the fifth chakra is called Vishuddha in Sanskrit, meaning "purification." It is associated with communication and gives a voice to the lower chakras. Its colour is blue. When you struggle to speak your truth, drinking red clover, sage, peppermint, or anise tea can be helpful. Red clover, lemon balm and eucalyptus tea are also good.

Third Eye Chakra: Ajna

The sixth chakra, also known as the third eye chakra, is represented by the colour blue and is called Ajna in Sanskrit. Located between the eyebrows slightly above eye level, it is associated with perception, intuition, insight, and self-awareness. One way to open the Third Eye and tap into our sixth sense is through drinking Mugwort tea. This herbal infusion has properties that can enhance our dreams and help us connect with our intuition. It also heightens our imagination and allows us to visualize more vividly, opening spiritual dimensions of perception for healing. Mint, lemon, jasmine tea is also good.

Crown Chakra: Sahasrara

The Seventh chakra which is the crown chakra is called Sahasrara. It derives its name from the Sanskrit word meaning "thousandfold" and is situated at the highest point of your head. It is represented by the colour white. The crown chakra serves as a spiritual guide, allowing us to tap into our intuitive abilities. It is often represented by the sound "aum," which symbolizes the beginning of all things and the creation of the universe. One effective method for balancing this chakra is by drinking tea infused with herbs and flowers such as lavender, gotu kola, and Tulsi leaf. These ingredients have been known to enhance and guide our connection to spirituality.

Chapter 11

Tea / Coffee Meditation

*Mediation is a vital way to purify and quiet
the mind, thus rejuvenating the body.*
Deepak Chopra

What Is Meditation?

Meditation can be described as a practice of focusing one's
mind and being fully present in the current moment. Early
references to meditation known as dhyana can be traced back
to the *Upanishads*. The first recorded evidence of meditation
dates to 1500 BC in India, within the Hindu tradition known
as Vedantism. However, it is believed that the practice of
meditation existed even earlier, possibly as early as 3000 BC.
This practice holds significance in Hinduism, Jainism, and
Buddhism.

Throughout the Middle Ages, meditation evolved and gained
popularity as a form of prayer across various traditions. In the
18th century, there was an increasing interest in the ancient
practice among Western cultures. In 1927, the publication of
the *Tibetan Book of the Dead* captured the attention of many
Westerners and sparked curiosity about meditation. This led to
the emergence of insight meditation in Burma during the 1950s
known as the Vipassana movement. The book *The Dharma Bums*
was published in 1958 and further piqued interest in meditation
at that time.

Meditation

At first, I struggled with meditation. My mind was constantly
buzzing with thoughts and worries, making it difficult to

relax and let go. I felt overwhelmed and frustrated by my inability to quiet my mind. However, during my training as a Hypnotherapist, I learned that the key to achieving true relaxation is to stop resisting and simply be present in the moment. Now, I make it a habit to meditate twice a day – once in the morning and again before bed. If you're not used to meditating regularly like I am, it may be challenging to find the time and motivation. But I've found that when I make it a consistent part of my routine, it becomes easier and more beneficial for me.

Before You Meditate

When beginning a meditation practice, it is common to feel uneasy or unsettled by certain emotions and physical sensations. This does not mean that anything is wrong; in fact, it can be a sign that your mind is settling and becoming more aware. As you quiet the chaos in your mind, suppressed feelings may come to the surface. These are all normal experiences during meditation, so do not be alarmed.

There is no right or wrong way to meditate. It must be your way. Ease yourself into meditation slowly and as you complete this on a regular basis, it will become easier for you to do this. If you are listening to guided meditations, for example, I must listen to a soothing voice. I can highly recommend Jason Stephenson and *Rising Higher Meditation* and can be found on YouTube. Both are Australian and have a wealth of experience.

To start you on your path of meditation, why not try a tea or coffee meditation. In 2008, researchers from Yale discovered that feeling physical warmth can also lead to emotional warmth towards others. Participants in the study who held a cup of hot coffee were more inclined to believe that others were kind and compassionate, while those who held a warm therapeutic pad were more likely to choose gifts for friends instead of themselves. (*Experiencing Physical Warmth Promotes Interpersonal Warmth* – PMC nih.gov)

Tea / Coffee Meditation

The process of making a cup of tea or coffee for meditation goes beyond just boiling water and playing soothing music. It can be a form of meditation. Each stage, from choosing the ideal cup to savouring the final sip, can be approached with mindfulness and purpose.

How to Do a Tea/Coffee Meditation

- Put your phone on silent mode. You may want to play some soothing meditation music.
- Choose a coffee or tea of your choice. During this exercise, I always use loose tea as it keeps me in the present moment.
- Choose your cup, which one calls out to you? This could be a favourite one that you can use for this exercise.
- Pour fresh water into the kettle. Take note of the water boiling. Take a deep breath in through your nose and out of your mouth. Settle into a comfortable position and enjoy the moment.
- Allow the water to cool for a few minutes. Close your eyes again and use this time to take a breath in through the nose and out of your mouth.
- Pour the heated water into your cup. Listen to the sound as it touches the tea or coffee. What sounds can you hear?
- As you make your drink, breathe in through your nose and out of your mouth.
- Pause for a few minutes and allow the coffee or tea to release its flavour.
- Sit down and get comfortable.

- Give thanks for the cup of drink that is in front of you right now.
- In your hands, feel the warmth of the cup. Hold the cup to your nose and take a deep inhale before taking your first sip.
- How does it feel around your hand? Is the surface warm or has it already cooled down a bit.
- Start playing attention to your breath.
- Breath in through your nose. Hold for one second. Breath out of your mouth.
- Continue your calm breathing but now shift your focus to the coffee or tea in front of you.
- Continue with a peaceful and clam breath.
- How does the cup feel against your hands?
- Take another five breaths through your nose and out of your breath.
- Lift the cup in front of your face, breath in through your nose and blow out through your mouth. Concentrate on the aroma of the coffee/tea and take five cycles of your breath.
- Close your eyes. What can you smell? Is it sweet? Strong?
- Slowly bring the cup to your lips and take the first sip. Focus on your breathing and the sensations from the drink in your mouth and body.
- Lower the cup; but continue holding it in your hand. Concentrate again on your breath. Take five cycles of your breath.
- Continue to enjoy your drink, sip by sip. Savour each sip while being in the present moment with your drink and your body.
- When you are at your last sip of the hot drink, allow yourself to become more aware of your surroundings. Bring you awareness back to your breath... feel you're

in and out breaths as they continue to move through and around your body... feel your hands, arms, feet, legs, your head, your mind, your heart and let your breath guide you back to a full conscious awareness of yourself.

- Record your experiences in your journal.

Chapter 12

Keeping a Journal

*Journaling is like whispering to oneself
and listening at the same time.*
Mina Murray

What Is Journaling?

What do Samuel Pepys, Leonardo da Vinci, Oprah Winfrey, Richard Branson, Lady Gaga, Marie Curie and Albert Einstein all have in common? Each of these famous figures kept a journal/diary to record openly their personal thoughts, ideas, and musings. Ancient philosophers like Aristotle and Socrates kept an ongoing account of their lives. From self-help blogs to famous authors like Deepak Chopra, this has form of writing been around for thousands of years.

Journaling is a written account of your personal thoughts, insights, and feelings. It is one of the most powerful self-improvements at your fingertips that can assist you with your emotional well-being and is a deeply personal experience that can take many forms.

I have always kept a journal/diary during my childhood. I started around the age of eight, squirreling away my inner thoughts in one of those diaries with a padlock and key. I wrote about events of the day, and it became a way of expressing feelings and emotions. My diary/journal became a close friend.

I love journaling as there are not any rules as it can be written, drawn, even typed. Today, my journal is like a dialogue with my inner life where I can write down my goals and respond effectively to challenges that I am facing in my life.

Journaling allows you even to free write or even jot down in bullet points or even make a to-do list accompanied with doodles. Whatever your preference, Journaling is a low-cost way of improving your own mental health and well-being.

From my own experiences, it can be daunting to get started. It can feel like a chore, especially when you have agreed to do it every day. The trick is when starting this is to do little and often. Setting a timer for just five minutes can help you start with the positive effects of journaling. When you have reached this goal, why not increase it by a minute each week. By doing this, it encourages you to write longer and often.

During my tasseography readings, I have always kept a journal and record what I have discovered in each session. Tasseography readings serves as a great tool that can also help validates and increases your intuition. From my own experiences, this is a practical and effective way to incorporate this into your lives. A tasseography journal need not just be a place where you record your readings. It can also use to meditate and elaborate upon the symbols you see in the readings. It also provides you a safe space for you to record all intuitive and creative musings. This experience that can nourish you emotionally, mentally, creativity and spiritually.

Benefits of Journaling

The results of journaling are powerful. Here are just some of the benefits of keeping a journal.

- Improves mental health and well-being.
- Encourages and gain Self-Confidence.
- Helps with setting and achieving goals.
- Inspires Creativity.
- Track progress and inner growth.
- Reduce stress and anxiety.

- Find inspiration.
- Give you a place to express gratitude.
- Assists you with life challenges.

How to Keep a Journal

Journaling is an inexpensive relaxation exercise and you do not require a lot of equipment to get started with. You can use a notebook, a laptop or even a note-taking app to record your thoughts. The only way to gain the rewards that come with journaling is to be consistent. I also keep a 'Gratitude Journal'. Before going to sleep, each night, I write down three things that I am grateful for the day, week, and month. It is best if you weave your tasseography journal practice into your daily routine. This routine will keep you connected with your intuition and empower you.

I always note the date and time when reflecting on the reading. When recording your tasseography reading, record anything that may arise. Also take a note of your emotional being. There may be days when you feel overwhelmed, the key is to be kind to yourself. Write anything that presents itself.

There is no wrong or right way to choose your journal. Whatever works best for you is the best way.

After you have taken the time with your tasseography journal, it can enhance and help you clear your head, make important connections between thoughts, feelings, and emotions. Journalling is essentially a creative evolution and can lead to consistent written reflection. This form of self-expression could introduce you to parts of yourself that you didn't exist.

Keeping a journal is the best way to develop your mastery over the art of tasseography. Keeping a journal allows you to develop your dictionary of symbols, which reveal special meanings that only apply to you and can't be found in books. By the time you completely acquaint yourself with the symbols and tasseography, you will be able to see deeper meanings, and connections between the unfolding of situations; discover underlying patterns and solutions to problems. Through consistent journaling, you can establish a strong and personal relationship with yourself and your intuition and tasseography journaling enhance your communication with the symbols.

Chapter 13

How to Make Your Own DIY Brew

Afternoon tea should be provided, fresh supplies, with thin
bread-and-butter,fancy pastries, cakes, etc., being brought
in as other guests arrive.
Isabella Beeton, Mrs Beeton's Book
of Household Management

A Hot Cuppa

A hot cuppa of your choice is a great comforter especially on chilly evenings. Herbal iced tea and iced coffee are lovely to enjoy when you are looking for something completely different. From my own experiences, I have often used a homemade strong herbal iced tea as a mixer for cocktails and mocktails.

I am an avid tea drinker. I have consumed a lot of different tea blends and learned what I enjoy and what I need to avoid. There are a variety of herbal tea blends, tea blending kits, coffee blending kits available for purchase from websites and high street shops. Commercial blends use artificial flavourings, and you can avoid this by making your own blends in workshops.

Tea Blending Workshops

Bird & Blend hold themed tea tasting and blending workshop experiences running across the UK including London, Bristol, Glasgow and many more. Led by the UK's mixologist, you'll start by learning the ins and outs of tea: how they're made, how they're best enjoyed and their various health benefits. I got to sample an array of award-winning teas and you get a feel for flavours before you set about some blending of your own. On your arrival at your pre-booked session, you'll meet your expert tea mixologist who will chat to you about the ingredients you'll be using on the day. It was a magical experience for me. I got to create three blends of my own blends, designed, named, and packed by own very hands. What is good about these workshops, there is unlimited tea and tea cocktails throughout the workshop to help inspire you. And the best thing is that you take home your blends to make delicious tea at home. I recommend this magical day to anyone who is keen on tea. (*Tea Blending & Tasting Workshop Experiences* Bird & Blend Tea Co. birdandblendtea.com)

Coffee-Infused Beer

The combination of coffee and beer has been a popular experiment in the craft industry for some time now. From classic cold brew to nitro cold brew, even coffee wine has been explored as a new way to enjoy these beverages. Craft breweries have incorporated coffee into both lager and ale styles to enhance the flavour. While stouts and porters are commonly used as the base for coffee beer, many are branching out and trying different styles like cream ales and India pale ales. Despite containing caffeine, the amount is usually quite low. Brewers typically use a higher ratio of beer to coffee because their product is primarily labelled as a beer. For those who enjoy both coffee and alcohol, coffee beer with an alcohol content of around 4–5% and minimal caffeine can be a refreshing choice after a long day.

Mushroom Coffee

Mushroom coffee has gained popularity as a healthier substitute for traditional coffee. This trend has exploded on TikTok, with users claiming that it tastes just like regular coffee without the negative effects of caffeine. Many have even made videos showcasing their daily routine starting with a cup of mushroom coffee. However, upon further research I've found that this trendy coffee can also come with a hefty price tag. The taste is quite like regular coffee. There are various options available for purchase such as mushroom coffee grounds, pre-made lattes, and instant pods. The most used mushrooms in these blends include: Reishi, Chaga, Lion's mane, and Cordyceps.

Rachel Patterson

Rachel Patterson is a Witch, High Priestess, published Author and Elder at the Kitchen Witch School. For more information on Rachel, please go to: www.rachelpatterson.co.uk

Here are some recipes she kindly shared with me.

Lemon & Mint Tea

Ingredients:
Handful of lemon balm (Melissa officinalis) leaves (washed)
Sprig of mint leaves
Teaspoon of honey
½ pint boiling water

Method: Pour hot water onto the leaves and allow too steep for five minutes then strain and add a teaspoon of honey. This can be drunk hot or chill in the fridge and add ice cubes for a refreshing cool drink.

Magic of the ingredients:
Lemon balm – success, love and healing
Peppermint – love, healing, purification, psychic powers
Honey – Happiness, healing, love, prosperity, passion, spirituality, faerie

Psychic Boost Chai

Ingredients:
Black tea – loose or in a teabag

Half a cinnamon stick or half a teaspoon of ground cinnamon
Half a teaspoon ground nutmeg
Pinch saffron
½ pint milk or coconut milk
Teaspoon honey

Method: Put all the ingredients into a saucepan and simmer for 5 to 10 minutes. Serve warm.

Magic of the ingredients:
Nutmeg – luck, money, health
Cinnamon – success, healing, power, love, protection
Saffron – happiness, energy, psychic powers, healing, fertility
Coconut – protection, purification, chastity
Honey – Happiness, healing, love, prosperity, passion, spirituality, faerie
Tea – Meditation, courage, strength, prosperity
Milk – spirituality, love.

Bubble Tea

Have you heard of bubble tea? I hadn't until my 11-year-old football mad daughter introduced me to this after watching many videos on TikTok and YouTube. Bubble tea is also known as *boba* or *pearl milk tea* has gained popularity around the world. Did you know that there's even been a recent Google doodle dedicated to it.

Bubble Tea is a Taiwanese drink which isn't new and is said to have been first introduced created in the 1980s. There are many theories who invented this beverage. Some state it is the brainchild of Liu Han-chieh who began serving the cold beverage at his teahouse. Others claim that Tu Tsong-ho was the creator of this drink. Although the true inventor is still debated, what I do know is that bubble tea was invented in Taiwan.

What Is Bubble Tea?

Bubble tea is a cold drink made with black tea, milk, sweetener like sugar and ice. The 'bubbles' are tapioca pearls known as boba and are small, chewy. The pearls are made by combining tapioca starch or flour, water, and brown sugar.

A few of my clients have asked me to read the bubbles. It can be carried out, yet I like to add it is a conventional way to read a cup and prefer to use tea leaves or coffee grinds. Bubble tea shops are all around the world. You can also buy kits from the internet to create your own bubble tea in the comfort of your home.

Coffee Blend Kits

For those who appreciate a good cup of coffee, single-origin coffees and coffee blends are probably familiar terms. Coffee blend kits offer an opportunity to explore different flavour profiles. These kits typically include samples of beans from four distinct regions, providing a chance to experiment and discover new tastes. By blending beans from various origins, you can unlock a world of complex flavours. Using whole beans and grinding them at home ensures a more consistent result than using pre-ground coffee.

Growing Your Own Herbal Tea Garden

The study of herbal medicine goes back thousands of years and the use of plants for healing and wellness. Herbs are part of many traditional systems of medicine around the world, such as Chinese and Ayurvedic.

From my own experiences buying herbs from the supermarket, markets and the internet can turn very expensive. When I started making my own tea blends, I opted for dried herbs which I always have in my kitchen cupboards. It was during the lockdown when I started to grow my own herbs from seeds. It was exciting to do this as I learned very quickly that using fresh herbs added more flavour sensation to my teas.

From my own experiences, homegrown herbs such as Mint, Lemon Balm and Chamomile are more potent than you would buy fresh from any supermarket. Basil, Oregano, Chives, Rosemary, and Lavender are easy to grow at home.

I started with buying indoor herb garden kits as I had everything that I needed to grow my own herb garden. The great thing about growing your own herbs is that they don't need to be grown in a garden. I have tubs of Mint, Sage, Rosemary, and Oregano which have lasted me for years and has become an amazing investment for when I make my own teas. If you decide to grow herbs in pots, they need to be at least ten inches in diameter, as the herbs need space to grow.

I found it satisfying going to the garden and cutting the herbs that I need to make my own tea blends. I got the best results from buying herb plants from a reputable garden centre and grow the plants from seed. Every year in March I start sowing the seeds myself in pots with moist peat-free compost and sprinkle the seeds of choice into them. I have discovered that when I cover each pot with clingfilm it helps the seeds to germinate into seedlings. In five weeks, I then thin out the herbs and replant them into separate pots which give me lots of fresh herbs.

As I hear the kettle reaching its boiling point, I grab my scissors and eagerly begin snipping fresh herbs. Before using them in my tea, I take care to rinse them lightly, ensuring that there are no unwanted insects or dirt that could spoil the flavour. Then, I place the fragrant herbs into a teapot and pour hot water over them, making sure it is just off-the-boil to prevent any essential oils from evaporating. After all, these herbs contain valuable oils that can be extracted to create essential oils.

Please Note: If you need to seek medical advice before embarking on making home-made teas, you should consult a doctor or other appropriate medical professional.

Nettle Tea

Nettles and Dandelions can be the bane of gardener's lives. Nettles are known for the stinging hairs on its leaves or stems. Various cultures around the globe have utilized Nettle Leaf (Urtica diocia) as a crucial component in traditional medicine for centuries.

Nettles can be found in Europe, North Africa, and Asia. Nettles were widely used throughout the Mediterranean region in Greek and Roman times. Roman soldiers rubbed it on themselves to help stay warm. Ancient Egyptians used nettles to treat arthritis and lower back pain. Nettles was the Anglo-Saxon sacred herb *wergula* and in medieval times nettle beer was drunk for rheumatism.

You can buy nettles as a dry leaf or freeze-dried. It can also be found in tablets and juices. Modern day science has found ways to use ancient beliefs about nettle's medicinal effects. Nettle tea have been used to help with joint pain, anaemia, and eczema.

Dandelion Tea

The word dandelion comes from the French word 'dent de lion' meaning lion's tooth because of the jagged shape of the leaves. Dandelion (Taraxacum officinale) are native to Asia and Europe. The dandelion has been recorded in ancient writings and Arabian physicians used the plant medicine in the tenth and eleventh centuries. For centuries, the Chinese and Indians have grown the dandelion to treat liver diseases and digestive problems. Dandelion is known in Traditional Chinese Medicine for its ability to reduce heat (inflammation) and aid the body in eliminating toxins. It was used in Europe in remedies for fever, boils, eye problems, diabetes, and diarrhoea. The Cherokee used it as a toothache remedy. William Cole, a 17th century herbalist, documented that dandelions have several benefits which were for the liver, gall, and spleen as well as treatment for jaundice.

Dandelion-and-burdock is a popular fizzy drink made in the North of England. I also like the aniseed flavour. It was originally a type of light mead but over the years it has evolved into the carbonated soft drink. Now you can buy this in teabags from high street shops in the United Kingdon. It promotes good digestion and is also a powerful as general tonic for the whole body and for those who have eczema-like conditions.

There are not many documented side effects from drinking this tea. Dandelion tea is made from flower petals. From my own experiences it has a sweet taste. Roasted dandelion root teas have a robust flavour. My Nan, Phyl, told me that if you picked dandelions, it would make you wet the bed. There may be some truth in this because. dandelion tea should not be drunk before bed as it is diuretic, and you don't want to be in the bathroom all night. It is suggested that you talk to your medical professional before adding dandelion tea to your daily life, especially if you have kidney problems, are on medications are pregnant or nursing.

Spruce Tea

Spruces and pines have been used as food source for centuries during the lean months of winter. Spruce needles when harvested in the springtime it has a slight natural sweetness that from my own experience pairs well with lime and honey.

Spruce tea is traditionally used to combat scurvy, colds, coughs, and fatigue. The flavour of this tea will vary depending on the variety of tree the tips have been harvested from. If you have pine allergies, you should avoid drinking this tea because it could result in skin rashes, respiratory issues, nausea, or diarrhoea. The Yew tree should be avoided as it is highly toxic.

You can buy wild foraged spruce tip tea that is packed with vitamin C from online shops. It makes a potent cold remedy. It is made by brewing fresh or dried spruce needles.

Herbs to Grow

Here are some herbs that you can grow in your garden at home.

Mint

Mint has been around for centuries. The word Menthe is associated with the green nymph Minthe. In Moroccan culture, the tea is steeped with mint and green tea leaves and sugar and served at all times of the day. Native Americans made a tea from wild mint leaves to relieve an upset stomach. Greeks and Egyptians used peppermint as medicine. Chewing peppermint leaves is a Persian folk remedy for toothaches. In India, herbal mixtures containing peppermint treat indigestion, coughs, colds, and other ailments. Mint likes moist but well-drained soil. It can grow in full sun to partial shade. Mint is easy to grow but it is best to put it in a large pot on its own. I have used a bucket and sunk it into the ground, to keep its roots contained as I've discovered it can take over other herbs growing alongside it. There's also enormous range of mint that you can grow from Field mint (Mentha arvensis) Peppermint (Mentha x piperita) Spearmint (Mentha spicata) Apple mint, Banana mint, Grapefruit mint, Moroccan mint, Pineapple mint, Chocolate mint, Ginger mint, Lime mint, Strawberry mint. Water mint (Mentha aquatica) is an aquatic species for growing in ponds. This herb is an herbaceous perennial and dies back over winter and regrows every spring.

Using fresh mint leaves gives the tea a captivating herbal aroma and flavour. As this tea is made with an herb instead of tea leaves, it is considered as a tisane. A tisane (pronounced tea-zahn) is an infusion or decoction made from a plant. Tisanes are caffeine-free and can be severed hot or cold.

Lemon Balm

Lemon Balm is botanically known as Melissa officinalis and belongs to the mint family *Lamiaceae* and is easy to grow. Originating in the Middle East and North Africa, the herb was brought to Spain by the Moors in the 7th century. The genus name Melissa means 'bee' in Greek. The plant was named for its ability to attract bees. First century Roman naturalist Pliny the Elder, wrote that lemon balm planted near bee hives would encourage them to return. The word balm is derived from the Greek word *balsamon* which means balsam. Dioscorides, a first century Greek physician wrote that lemon balm would promote menstruation, improve gout, remedy toothaches and if mixed with wine, could be used to treat scorpion stings and dog bites. The Greeks and Romans used it medicinally and information about lemon balm was recorded as 300 BC in Theophrastus's Historia Plantarum

Research in 2021 suggests that lemon balm may benefit mood and cognitive performance. The study demonstrated that treatment with lemon balm led to improvements in tasking involving memory, concentration, and mathematics.

Please Note: If you are taking sedatives for insomnia or anxiety, please check with your doctor before taking lemon balm tea.

People use lemon balm tea to help improve mood, slow cognitive decline, and decrease anxiety levels. Growing lemon balm from my own experiences is easy to grow from seed. You can buy ready-grown varieties as plants from all good garden centres.

The soil needs to rich and well-drained and likes a sunny spot in the garden. You can control the spreading by cutting back flowering stems in late summer.

Chamomile

Chamomile has been used in teas, skincare, and haircare. The earliest recorded use of this herb for medical purposes was in 1550 BC. and featured in Eber's Papyrus – an Egyptian medical papyrus of herbal knowledge. The Greeks and Egyptians used crushed chamomile flowers to treat the skin conditions erythema an xerosis caused by dry, harsh weather. It was recorded in the 10th century as one of the nine sacred herbs of the *Lacnunga*, an ancient Anglo-Saxon herbal manuscript. In Rome it was often used to treat headaches. Chamomile tea was used in the Middle Ages in Europe as a diuretic and a tonic to manage pain and fatigue.

Chamomile is easy to grow from seed which can be sown in the spring. There are chamomile plants that you can buy which may be named varieties of the herb. They like plenty of sun and light soil that drains freely which doesn't dry out or get waterlogged. It is an annual plant that comes back every year.

Rosemary

Rosemary is derived from the Latin name *Rosmarinus* meaning 'dew of the sea.' This herb was used as an incense in cultural ceremonies and spiritual rituals for thousands of years. The ancient Greeks believed that Rosemary was a gift from Aphrodite, Goddess of love and frequently appeared at weddings. Rosemary was extremely popular in Europe and was thought to have power to prevent negativity from entering a house and people would tuck Rosemary under their pillows to ward of bad dreams and evil spirits.

Rosemary (*Salvia Rosmarinus*) has a pungent aroma and is originally from mediterranean climates, this herb is a hardy plant through most of the United Kingdom. This herb is easy to grow and look after. My plants thrive in a sunny, sheltered spot in well-drained soil. I have had no luck in growing Rosemary from seed. It is best to buy small plants from a garden centre. This herb requires little attention. Don't forget to prune the plants in the autumn to keep plants to the size of the garden or they will grow out of control.

Sage

The name sage comes from the Latin salvo (to save or heal). This herb is associated with Jupiter and was thought by the Romans to strengthen the memory and promote wisdom. Sage has been associated with immortality, chewing sage has been created in mythology to increase mental capacity. For centuries, sage has been employed to enhance the radiance of refined women.

Many people in China used this herb to treat colds, joint pain, typhoid fever, kidney, and liver issues. Sage is native to the Mediterranean region. Botanically known as *Salvia Officinalis* and comes from the Latin word 'salvere' meaning 'to be saved.'

Sage also belongs to the mint family. There are many different types of sage herb to choose from. From my own experiences, Sage prefers a warm sheltered position in full sun. You can also grow sage in pots. You can cut the leaves as and when you need them. Trim the perennial types of sage after flowering.

Thyme

Thyme was used by the ancient Egyptians for embalming. The ancient Greeks used it in their baths and burnt it as incense in their temples. Romans used this herb as a flavouring for cheese and alcoholic beverages. It was also apparently offered it as a cure people for who were melancholic or shy. The Roman army introduced thyme to the British Isles when they invaded. Hippocrates recommended this herb for respiratory diseases and conditions. In the 1340's the Black Death took hold of

Europe, people would wear posies of thyme for protection. Botanically know as *Thymus Vulgaris*.

Thyme seeds are best sown in the spring. Thyme is evergreen, and you can pick sprigs all year round. New growth in spring and summer gives the best flavour for tea. Thyme tea is good for relieving ailments such as colds, flu, and tonsillitis. Thyme is rich in Phenol which is a powerful antiseptic. Taking too much of this tea can act as a diuretic and cause dehydration, headaches, and dizziness.

Chapter 14

Tea Recipes

Brewing your own tea may seem daunting, but it's simpler than you realise. Making your own blends of tea is simple and more cost-effective than purchasing pre-made bags from the supermarket or online. It can also serve as a unique and charming gift option. Creating your own unique tea blends has never been simpler. Not only is it an easy process, but it allows for endless flavour combinations and the chance to discover your personal favourites. As a Tea Herbalist, I have compiled a list of my favourite recipes that I would love to share with you.

The Benefits of Blending Your Own Tea

With just a few simple ingredients, such as pure teas and various herbs, flowers, and spices, you can create many different blends and enjoy a new tea every day. Even small changes in the ingredients can completely transform a tea's taste and effects. Blending is also useful for improving the flavour of teas that may not be your favourite but have health benefits you want to reap. You can easily find the necessary ingredients in health food stores or even grow your own herbs and collect flowers or fruits to dry. This way, you can avoid the added sugars or artificial flavours often found in pre-made blends.

The Basics of Blending

To create a well-balanced tea blend, a base ingredient is crucial. This can be a pure tea or dried herb that serves as the foundation for all the other flavours to blend. For a revitalising summer beverage, incorporating fresh herbs like mint and spearmint with tangy fruits such as lemon, hibiscus, and strawberries makes for an invigorating combination. In contrast, during the colder months, spices are the perfect choice to create a comforting and warming tea. From my own experimentation with blending teas, I have found that black and Rooibos teas complement sweet ingredients, while green tea enhances sour, fruity, and earthy flavours.

PLEASE NOTE: Although I make every effort to be completely precise, it is ultimately the responsibility of the reader to confirm the correct identification of plants. The information given is not intended or implied to be a substitute for professional medical advice, diagnosis, or treatment.

It's important to be cautious when consuming wild plants, as some can be toxic and have serious negative effects on one's health. Please note that I am **NOT** a medical or nutritional professional nor a doctor. It is the responsibility of the reader to seek verification from qualified experts regarding nutritional information and potential health benefits of any edible plants mentioned.

Always seek the advice of your physician or other qualified health care provider with any questions you may have regarding a medical condition or treatment and before undertaking a new health care regimen, and never disregard professional medical advice or delay in seeking it because of something you have read in this book.

Tea Blend Tips

If you want to create your own unique tea blends, here are some recipes to get you started. These recipes serve as guidelines and suggestions for blending, using enough leaves for two or three infusions depending on the recipe. They feature popular herbs, fruits, and spices for easy blending. Keep in mind that each ingredient has its own nuances and strengths, so it's important to adjust the amounts according to your personal taste.

Additionally, the intensity of each ingredient can vary based on factors such as type, quality, and storage conditions. It's best to start with small batches and experiment before making larger quantities.

To make the strongest tea, also known as *infusing*, steep herbs in boiling water. It is recommended to steep them for a minimum of fifteen minutes before straining them out. The brewed tea can be kept in the fridge for up to two days without losing its medicinal properties. Using fresh herbs will require a larger quantity to achieve a flavourful brew; typically, three times more than using dried herbs. A standard tea uses one teaspoon of primary dried herb and ½ teaspoon of secondary dried herb per cup. For added taste, consider incorporating other ingredients such as dried fruit like apples, mangoes, apricots and spices like cinnamon, ginger, black pepper or add honey for a touch of sweetness.

Method

For those unfamiliar with blending herbs, this approach serves as a useful guide to help you get started.

1. When creating your own tea blend, it is important to consider herbal synergy. Begin by identifying the desired herbal action, such as immune support or calming effects. Use your preferred herb as the main ingredient base, as this will make up 70 to 80 percent of the blend. Most medicinal blends are made up of herbs that directly target a specific health concern. These primary herbs play a crucial role in achieving the desired results.

2. Include a "supportive herbal ingredient" known for its ability to provide relief and lessen the impact of more potent herbs. These supportive herbs typically make up 20 to 30 percent of the blend in herbal remedies.

3. The last crucial element is the "catalyst," which adds a burst of taste or enhances the potency of the active ingredient by complementing its actions. These herbs are only used in small quantities, making up around 5 to 10 percent of the blend. They have a warming or stimulating effect on the body and help to activate the tea's properties. Commonly used catalysts include ginger, peppermint, and cinnamon.

Please keep in mind that the ratios mentioned are not fixed, but rather flexible. Feel free to get creative and try different combinations. I personally prefer starting with three parts active ingredient, one to two parts supportive herbs, and quarter to one part catalyst. However, feel free to adjust as needed for your desired results.

Recipes

Rooibos and Pear Tea

Prep: 5 minutes
Cook: 6 minutes
Total: 11 minutes

Elevate your Rooibos tea by adding in fresh slices of pear and a cinnamon stick for a flavourful twist. For an extra touch, use additional pear slices as garnish.

Ingredients:
1 sliced ripe pear
½ a cinnamon stick
2 tsp rooibos leaf tea

Method: In a saucepan, combine the pear slices with 600ml of water and a cinnamon stick. Set aside a few slices for later use as decoration. Bring the mixture to a simmer and let the pears cook for five to six minutes until they begin to soften. Remove the pan from the heat and add in the rooibos tea. Allow the mixture too steep for two to three minutes before transferring it into a warmed teapot. For an extra touch, garnish with additional pear slices before serving.

Fresh Mint Tea

Prep: 5 minutes
Cook: 5 minutes
Total: 10 minutes

For the best taste, use fresh mint when making this tea. It has a bright and refreshing flavour that is perfect for enjoying after meals. This delicious Fresh Mint Tea is simple to prepare and will leave you feeling satisfied.

Ingredients:
Fresh mint – 2 sprigs – Spearmint and peppermint both work well.
1 ½ cups Water (350 ml)
1 slice Lemon (optional)
1 teaspoon Honey (optional) – For a slightly sweeter tea, serve it with a drizzle of honey mixed in.

Method: First, you'll need to bring some water to a boil. This can be done in a kettle or on the stove. Once the water has reached a rolling boil, pour it into your serving glasses. Next, take a few sprigs of fresh mint and gently roll them between your hands to release their oils. Add one or two sprigs to each glass and let them steep for three to five minutes. If desired, you can also add a drizzle of honey and stir until it dissolves. For an extra touch of flavour, garnish with a slice of lemon and squeeze in some lemon juice. A helpful tip: You can also enjoy this tea iced by refrigerating it before serving over ice. Or, if you prefer black tea, simply add fresh mint leaves to hot black tea for a refreshing twist.

Camomile Tea with Honey

For a wonderfully calming tea, mix dried chamomile flowers, fragrant lavender, and honey. This blend is great for starting your day off on a soothing note or for winding down at night.

Prep: 5 minutes
Cook: 5 minutes
Total: 5 minutes

Ingredients:
2 tsp dried chamomile flowers
Pinch dried lavender (optional)
Honey (optional)

Method: In a teapot, combine chamomile and lavender before filling it with boiled water. Allow the herbs too steep for two to three minutes. Stir in honey, then pour into your cup.

Ginger and Honey Chamomile Tea

This comforting blend of chamomile, honey and fresh ginger tea is exactly what you need, even if you didn't realise it. It's not only a delicious treat, but also a balm for your soul. Whether I'm feeling stressed, tired, or under the weather, this tea never fails to bring me comfort. With its simple ingredients of chamomile flowers, fresh ginger, honey, and lemon, it soothes with every sip. And it can be enjoyed warm or iced, making it perfect for any time of year.

Prep: 5 minutes
Cook: 5 minutes
Total: 10 minutes

Ingredients:
2 tsp dried chamomile flowers
Pinch dried lavender (optional)
Honey (optional)
Ginger

Method: In a teapot, combine ginger, chamomile, and lavender before filling it with boiled water. Allow the herbs too steep for four minutes. Stir in honey, then pour into your cup.

Chamomile-Honey Hot Toddy Recipe

A cozy hot toddy made with chamomile tea, honey, and your choice of whiskey, rum, or brandy. This soothing drink will help you drift off to sleep in no time as a perfect nightcap. I use a Chamomile tea bag for this recipe.

Ingredients:
2 tablespoons whiskey, bourbon, brandy, or dark rum
2 teaspoons fresh lemon juice
1 tablespoon honey
¼ cup boiling hot water or up to ½ cup, if you don't like it
    strong
1 chamomile tea bag
Lemon for garnish (optional)

Method: Combine your preferred alcohol, lemon juice, and honey in a small cup. Pour the mixture into a cup of hot water and stir until the honey blends in completely. Next, add the chamomile tea bag and let it soak for a few minutes. If desired, remove the tea bag before serving. Serve hot with a side of lemon to squeeze in as desired.

Resources

Jason Stephenson – www.jasonstephenson.net

For over 15 years, Jason has studied the positive effects of guided meditation and relaxation music. His YouTube channels – *Jason Stephenson Sleep Meditations* and *Relax and Recharge by Jason Stephenson* has grown to over 4.5 million subscribers, with over 1 billion views combined.

Jess Shepherd – www.jessshepherd.com

Rising Higher Meditation. Lift your vibration, align with your inner being and manifest magnificence.

Bird and Blend – www.birdandblendtea.com

Bird and Blend have themed tea tasting and blending workshop experiences running across the United Kingdom including London, Bristol, Glasgow and many more. Choose from their range of workshops including Tea Blending, Cocktail Tea Mixology & Magical Potions Tea Blending.

Teas for Bees – www.teasforbees.co.uk

Teas for Bees offers a variety of herbal teas, all made from natural ingredients grown on their farm. They have over 50 different options to choose from, including peppermint, spearmint, lemon verbena, and more unique flavours like chocolate, apple, and mojito mint. You can purchase pre-mixed blends or create your own at a local market where you can meet the makers in person. Their blends feature hand-picked leaves, flowers, fruits, and roots such as elderflowers, rosemary, and haw berries. Some popular recipes include Rest and Digest with Moroccan mint and anise hyssop, and Winter Booster with rosehips, elderberries, and lavender buds. Take your pick and enjoy the taste of nature in every sip.

Tea Leaf Reading Cards – www.giftrepublic.com

With the assistance of these cards, you can easily master the ancient skill of reading tea leaves. Discover the different areas of the teacup and their significance, as well as common symbols and their interpretations, to gain insight into your future. This set includes 100 cards for maximum guidance.

Tea Leaf Fortune Cards – www.usgamesinc.com/ tea-leaf-fortune-cards.html

Featuring illustrations by Shawna Alexander, this set provides a unique approach to divination with 200 beautifully drawn cards featuring traditional tea leaf symbols. The accompanying guidebook, consisting of 98 pages, explains how to use the tea leaf cards for fortune-telling or traditional tea leaf reading methods. The contents include a brief history of tea and tea leaf reading, the origins of Tea Leaf Fortune Cards, as well as instructions on how to use the cards for divination purposes through various methods such as the Coming Year Method, the Coming Week Method, and the Astral House Pyramid Method. Additionally, there is a list of tea leaf symbols and their meanings. The author and artist, Rae Hepburn, is an experienced tea leaf reader who will teach you how to unlock the ancient secrets of reading tea leaves.

Bibliography

Fenton, Sasha *Teacup Reading: A Quick and Easy Guide to Tasseography.* Red Wheel / Weiser, 2002.

Fontana, Marjorie A. *Cup of Fortune: A Guide to Tea Leaf Reading.* Wis.: Fantastic, 1979.

Kent, Cicely. *Telling Fortunes by Tea Leaves.* 1922.

Posey, Sandra Mizumoto. *Cafe Nation: Coffee Folklore, Magick, and Divination.* Santa Monica: Santa Monica Press, 2000.

Sheridan, Jo. *Teacup Fortune-telling.* London: Mayflower, 1978.

O'Reilly, Annie. *Tea with Annie, a definitive guide to Tasseomancy and its artistry.* Melbourne: Whiteslaw Press, 2014.

O'Reilly, Roxy. *The Lady of the Cup.* Perth, Quality Press, 2009.

Yaman, Beytullah. *The Art of Turkish Coffee Brewing.* Ankara: Bilkent University Press, 1987.

Zawinski, A. (2010). Hearts and diamonds: Or the lesson of the gypsy tearoom in tasseography and cartomancy. *Paterson Literary Review, 38,* 60–61.

References

www.chopra.com/ccl/the-history-of-meditation

Experiencing Physical Warmth Promotes Interpersonal Warmth – PMC (nih.gov)

A Highland Seer. (circa 1881). *Teacup reading and fortune-telling by tea leaves, by a highland seer.* https://www.gutenberg.org/ebooks/18241

About Kylie

Kylie Holmes was brought into this world on October 31st, 1970, in Bedford. She grew up with her parents, younger sister, and brother in Bedfordshire. From a young age, Kylie showed a passion for writing and enjoyed creating her own stories. This sparked her love of reading and her admiration for Roald Dahl's work. As she grew older, she discovered fantasy author Neil Gaiman and considers *The Graveyard Book* to be one of her top picks. With a deep interest in science fiction, Kylie is particularly drawn to the concept of time travel.

Despite struggling with dyslexia, Kylie has faced many challenges head-on, including learning how to drive. She has held various jobs throughout her life, such as a bartender, secretary, and tennis coach. However, her favourite roles include creating children's books, inspiring others to pursue their writing passions, and being a single mother to her four children.

Alongside her natural intuition, Kylie has honed her skills through meditation, self-development techniques, and courses related to Mind-Body-Spirit practices. With over 30 years of experience in Meditation and Mindfulness teaching, as well as 20 years as a Hypnotherapist and Past Life Regression Therapist, she also holds certifications as a Tea Herbalist Practitioner and Spiritual Life Coach. Additionally, Kylie is a member of the Society of Children's Book Writers and Illustrators (SCWBI) and was awarded the Margaret Carey Scholarship in 2018.

Kylie received training at the College of Psychic Studies and is certified by Flavia Kate Peters as an *Angel Therapy Practitioner®* and *Fairy Therapy Practitioner®*. Drawing on her personal experiences with angelic connections, she offers workshops designed to help others connect with the Angelic realm and spirit guides while tapping into their own potential. In one-on-one consultations, Kylie uses her intuition to guide individuals through issues related to their career, relationships, health, and overall life path. Her direct yet compassionate approach helps clients feel confident, relaxed, and empowered.

When she's not writing or working with clients, you can find Kylie walking her Border collies or indulging in her love for ice cream and cheesecake.

For more details about Kylie, please go to:
www.touchedbyanangel.me.uk
www.kylieholmes.co.uk

MOON BOOKS
PAGANISM & SHAMANISM

What is Paganism? A religion, a spirituality, an alternative belief system, nature worship? You can find support for all these definitions (and many more) in dictionaries, encyclopedias, and text books of religion, but subscribe to any one and the truth will evade you. Above all Paganism is a creative pursuit, an encounter with reality, an exploration of meaning and an expression of the soul. Druids, Heathens, Wiccans and others, all contribute their insights and literary riches to the Pagan tradition. Moon Books invites you to begin or to deepen your own encounter, right here, right now.

If you have enjoyed this book, why not tell other readers by posting a review on your preferred book site.

Bestsellers from Moon Books
Pagan Portals Series

The Morrigan
Meeting the Great Queens
Morgan Daimler
Ancient and enigmatic, the Morrigan reaches out to us.
On shadowed wings and in raven's call, meet the ancient Irish
goddess of war, battle, prophecy, death, sovereignty, and magic.
Paperback: 978-1-78279-833-0 ebook: 978-1-78279-834-7

The Awen Alone
Walking the Path of the Solitary Druid
Joanna van der Hoeven
An introductory guide for the solitary Druid, The Awen Alone
will accompany you as you explore, and seek out your
own place within the natural world.
Paperback: 978-1-78279-547-6 ebook: 978-1-78279-546-9

Moon Magic
Rachel Patterson
An introduction to working with the phases of the Moon, what
they are and how to live in harmony with the lunar year and to
utilise all the magical powers it provides.
Paperback: 978-1-78279-281-9 ebook: 978-1-78279-282-6

Hekate
A Devotional
Vivienne Moss
Hekate, Queen of Witches and the Shadow-Lands, haunts the pages
of this devotional bringing magic and enchantment into your lives.
Paperback: 978-1-78535-161-7 ebook: 978-1-78535-162-4

Readers of ebooks can buy or view any of these bestsellers by clicking on the live link in the title. Most titles are published in paperback and as an ebook. Paperbacks are available in traditional bookshops. Both print and ebook formats are available online.

Find more titles and sign up to our readers' newsletter
www.collectiveinkbooks.com/paganism

For video content, author interviews and more, please subscribe to our YouTube channel.

MoonBooksPublishing

Follow us on social media for book news, promotions and more:

Facebook: Moon Books

Instagram: @MoonBooksCI

X: @MoonBooksCI

TikTok: @MoonBooksCI

Printed and bound by CPI Group (UK) Ltd, Croydon, CR0 4YY

07/01/2025

01816805-0005